WITH
PARENTHOOD

Contemporary
Dilemmas

Irwin Matus, Ph.D.

GYLANTIC PUBLISHING COMPANY
Littleton, Colorado

Although the author has extensively researched all information to ensure the accuracy and completeness of the information contained in this book, the author and publisher assume no responsibility for errors, inaccuracies, omissions or any other inconsistency herein. Data contained herein are the most complete and accurate available as this book goes to print. Please bear in mind that meanings can vary due to personal interpretation.

GYLANTIC PUBLISHING COMPANY
P.O. Box 2792
Littleton, Colorado 80161-2792
1-800-828-0113 Fax: 303-727-4279 Email: GylanP@aol.com
Please add $2.00 to each order for shipping and handling.

Printed in the United States of America by Gilliland Printing, Inc. The text is printed with soy ink.

Cover by Lehman Design

Copyright © 1995 by Irwin Matus, Ph.D.

Library of Congress Cataloging-in-Publication Data

Matus, Irwin, 1934-
    Wrestling with parenthood : contemporary dilemmas / Irwin Matus.
        p. cm.
    Includes index.
    ISBN 1-880197-12-X
    1. Parenthood. 2. Parents—Psychology. 3. Parenting—Case studies. I. Title.
HQ775.8.M37 1995
649 '. 1—dc20   94-41833
                                                                        CIP

For Marilyn—who left too soon

Note to the Reader

It is my intention not only to be gender unbiased, but to write in an easy to read manner. The convention of the generic "he" is rightfully outdated. In this section, I refer to actual people as they are. I refer also to generalized people. For the sake of convenience, I label a child as "he" and a parent as "she". This simplifies the text and also reflects that mothers are the more likely to be involved in the situations that I describe. It is therefore less confusing to refer to the child as "he." This does not rule out that fathers and daughters are also involved.

Table of Contents

Preface

Glancing skyward, a two year old notices a glowing round object. Awe-struck, he turns to ask, "Is the moon a cookie?" The delight in responding to my son's question tells me all I need to know about why I am a parent. His sincerity and innocence, totally disarming, generates a warmth and joyousness that is unique to a parent-child relationship. To think that my own seed has developed such a high level of accomplishment touches me. Dozens, perhaps hundreds of such incidents add up to an experience as profound as any to be encountered during the course of a lifetime. Yet, so much more of parenting is considerably less than profound. For as you get down to the specific nuts and bolts of child rearing, you find plenty of rather demeaning, low-level labor. The pressures are compounded by the problem of constructing a balanced life that keeps the agenda in line with what it was intended to be. One begins to find that the constraints of maintaining the nest frustrates and narrows options for many other compelling experiences. Now "we" are the older generation, no longer to be realized. The passage of yet another developmental milestone signals a step in our own decline.

The novelist, Somerset Maugham was interested in people to the point of marriage and family. That was, to him, the end of the story. His attention then turned to the succeeding generation. I wonder if thoughts such as these hover in the unconscious of many middle class couples who choose to curtail the size of their family or who opt to exclude parenting from the agenda.

Yet, parenting is the most central of life experience. It is with us from the moment we are born and encounter our own parents as lifelines and conduits of the human experience. The moment of realization, when a toddler announces that "when I grow up, I will be a mommy, daddy" taps into a very basic meaning of our existence. The period of fantasy play explores the possibilities of sex roles and adult potential. Later, sex-play inevitably leading to intercourse, teases the prospects of procreation. Dating and mating brings these prospects closer to realization. Even the renunciation of these prospects through life style or religious vows has meaning to the parenting role. The definition of oneself as non-parent is the other side of the parental coin. Prevention acknowledges the procreative potential. There is no escaping what fate has created for us.

Ironically, despite the central and profound aspects of the parent motif, the subject is so commonplace that it is likely to be treated most casually. Should a parent seek relief from a child-raising problem, she or he is likely to find discussions that assume a failure in technique or absence of information as a basic cause. If only the parent knew a bit more about behavioral management or child development, so that argument goes, the problem would be solved. This may be true in some cases. But more likely, the meshing of parent and child is so complex that matters of technique or information have little relevance. For without considering the baseline from which individual parenting experiences begin and without a framework for understanding a child's urges and resistances toward growth it is not really possible to be relevant. The baseline and the framework are destined to impact and to entwine in crucial ways. In an absence of understanding of these elements, the parenting experience is trivialized, the child's point of view is ignored and the ingredients for influencing positive change is lacking.

Accordingly, this book attempts to return to the basics. It asks, why do people have children? What is a good parent? Why do children grow-up or fail to grow-up psychologically. Inasmuch as these are simple-minded questions reminiscent of the precocious two year old, the book is dedicated to the "why stage of development." It is during that stage that the child first discovers the joy of intellectual curiosity. By asking about commonplace matters he begins to develop a truer and more realistic picture of the nature of things. That is my hope, too, in taking this approach.

My purpose in asking these questions goes beyond idle curiosity, however. In acknowledging that parenting is not only a profound experience, but an exceptionally difficult job, it will be possible to capture a fuller appreciation of the experience and of the problems. It is hardly an exaggeration to assert that flying to the moon is nothing in comparison with raising a child. Former astronaut James Irwin acknowledged as much upon entering the ministry.

"It's always tougher when you're dealing with human problems." he said, "It was easy to deal with technical things, switches and controls in a spacecraft—much easier than dealing with human problems." Preceding Mr. Irwin's trip to the moon, many rockets blew up on the launching pad and hosts of technical problems needed to be solved. Undoubtedly, the solution to these problems were signs of technical ingenuity. Yet, the mechanical troubleshooter is in a much better position to analyze and solve the problem than is the parent or counselor addressing a human problem. The mechanic has sets of tools and spare parts, knowledge of the function of components and sub-systems, blue prints and schematics to serve as guideposts. The human element is of no consequence. In contrast, the parent counselor works in relative darkness. The definition of a problem is not usually signaled by an event as dramatic as a rocket exploding on a launching pad. More likely, there is a history of minor disturbances leading a parent to conclude at some point that there is a problem. The child may not agree. In his or her eyes the parent is overreacting.

Without agreement that a problem exists, the motivation to solve it is lacking. For solving the problem entails a process of change, and, no matter how miserable a person may be, human nature resists change. Even if resistance is surmounted, it is difficult to locate the proper tools and spare parts to repair the difficulty. Supposing it is a matter of interpersonal chemistry; the child is temperamentally gregarious, the parent intolerant of noise. These may be qualities that are unchangeable. If change is possible, it requires direction. Without blueprints and schematics, it is not possible to delineate the direction of change. Furthermore, the process of seeking change is not objective and dispassionate. Hardly. The human element is emotional, defensive, contrary and self-serving. Is it too late to enroll in a program of aeronautical engineering?

Rather, this book proposes to appreciate the dimensions of parenting and then relate these to a framework for understanding psychological growth. By integrating these two realms of human experience an outlook and direction for troubleshooting growth problems is provided. Issues such as discipline or communication are not addressed as such. The book may be troubling because it proposes few answers and it acknowledges that some problems may be unsolvable. It recognizes the limits of parent influence, allowing, then, that our most sincere rescue fantasies may never be realized. But the purpose is not to extol despair. On the contrary, the book presents a framework from which strategies for recognizing and responding to problems for what they are can be derived. While not for everybody, the approach will likely appeal to those who prefer to think through problems and seek their own solutions.

The experiences of many people contributed to this book. Many allowed a peek into their parenthood through formal and informal interviews. Other information was derived from counseling and clinical files. Finally, I drew upon my personal experience as a parent in the hope that my family will enjoy learning that our life together is as a dream come true.

Acknowledgments

A psychologist has license to peek into all the corners of people's lives. I am responsible for setting the tone that enables the safety to explore dangerous emotional territory. I do not know the answers, but it helps to ask the right questions. I also listen and learn. My patients generated the ideas and perspectives about which I write. Thanks to all.

My therapist did for me what I try to do for others. Florine Berkowitz Livson possessed wonderful humanity. If she was alive, I'd thank her personally.

Many professors and supervisors provided support, encouragement and patience. They took a chance on an unconventional and aging student. I hope that on reading this book they will not regret their efforts.

Colleagues and friends gave freely of their time to read and comment upon the manuscript. I thank Tom Olkowski, Bill Van-Doornick, Laurie Swetnam-Wood, Barb Pagnano, Richard Thal, Essie Gooside, Bruce and Martha Hartman.

Sandi and Hal Goldberg, David Eisner, Jane Levitas, Ellen Silon and Steve Axelrath graciously allowed in-depth exploration of their private lives. Their contributions were invaluable.

Jordan, Seth, and Estelle are my family. Our life together provides the best and most meaningful moments for me. Without them, this book could not have been written.

Chapter 1

Procreating—Reasons and Motives

Would you in sound mind and clear judgment seek this position? Decide—do you really want an application? If you are a parent, it's too late. Life's most demanding job, the nuts and bolts of raising a child, is already yours. Working conditions are difficult—drudgery, unworthy of civilized, emancipated individuals. But call it parenting and the most menial, unrewarding tasks become joyous acts of love. Of all decisions made during a lifetime, none has a more far-reaching effect than the decision to have children. Para-

Help Wanted

No experience necessary. Mature, M/F for career position. Full-time commitment for three years with gradually decreasing time demands for next 15 years. Job demands substantial financial investment without guarantee of return. 24-hour, on-call availability. Successful candidate will function well under tight deadlines in hectic atmosphere. High tolerance for menial labor required. Applicants should enjoy learning about child development and willingly participate in child-related activities. Even temperament and pleasant disposition are desirable. Ability to supervise, train, impose appropriate discipline, mediate disputes, and tolerate abuse are necessary. Working conditions will vary. No salary. Rewards are not commensurate with experience and education. No opportunity for career advancement. People in their right minds need not apply. Equal opportunity posi-

doxically and despite the demands of the job, procreation remains as popular as ever.

The erosion of past role constraints and the easy availability of birth control have led to increased freedom and flexibility in living the good life. Yet, many couples still include children in that vision. Given the demands of child raising, the choice is astonishing. Parenting expresses the most profound and the most menial of human experience. It confuses the noblest with the most base of motivations.

Western culture and religious heritage convince us that as rational beings our choices reflect freedom of will. Tolerance and diversity in our society allow the construction of lives in accordance with inner ideals and preferences. While we are occasionally outraged by those who defy accepted standards and traditions, much room to innovate remains within these boundaries. We master our fate through reason, weighing consequences of possible loss against likely payoff. Or, do we?

A rational decision maker considers the impact of parenting. Clearly, parenting is not relevant to one who dedicates every waking moment to a singular passion or goal. Nor is it a reasonable decision without the means to handle the financial, social, and emotional responsibilities of raising a child. Knowing oneself determines the meaningfulness and emotional fulfillment of parenting. Romantic notions are important but they are unrealistic unless balanced by practical understanding. Given the impact of the decision, it is crucial to address difficult questions. Potential parents should weigh all the factors.

Consider the implications of a bad decision. There is no joy in procreation if parenting offers no emotional fulfillment. If having a child is not relevant to one's life agenda, the result can be unhappy and disastrous. Likewise, the unexpected demands of raising a child would be unpleasant to one harboring only the romantic illusions of child rearing. These miscalculations can turn a blessed event into a nightmare.

The premise that rational decision making should be part of the parenthood process is beyond argument. But even educated, sophisticated people can be irrational about bringing a child into the world. Virtuous decisions may be as faulty as bad ones. The idea that procreation creates immortality is deeply felt by many who seek to exist after death through the offspring's body and spirit. Yet, as Woody Allen said, the only way to be immortal is to live forever. Great sages have uttered immortal words. At best, such immortality lasts only a few thousand years, nothing compared to the age of the universe. The best genealogists trace ancestry back a few generations. Desire for immortality is not a rational point on which to choose procreation.

Other people choose to become parents to correct injustices suffered in their own childhood. The thought that such injustices can be undone and corrected by giving the new baby a better go of it is understandable, but it is not a rational reason to have a child. While this view can add purpose and dedication, the resolution of unfinished emotional business has nothing to do with parenting the new baby. The past cannot be recreated.

The decision to procreate includes rational and irrational elements. Without balance between the two, adverse results for parents and child are likely.

Some elements of irrationality can add good qualities to the decision: parental feelings and images, positive belief, playfulness, and opportunities to retouch one's own inner child. Other elements can be detrimental because they attempt to solve unrelated problems through pregnancy (reviewed later in this chapter). Conversely, rationality not only checks harmful irrational tendencies, but adds the ability to critically assess important elements of reality. The difference between creating a blessed event and a personal mess is determined by how well these two levels of thought mix.

Understanding the mixture of motivation, thought, and experience enables a parent to appreciate subtle qualities that enhance and impede the job of raising a child. Such understanding is the avenue for gaining control and maximizing satisfaction and functioning.

To simplify, procreation, parenting, and parenthood are differentiated.

- Procreation refers to the act of conceiving a child. The act, of course, is sexual and its motives and intentions are complex. Regardless, should conception result, an intense defining event with profound and lasting impact has occurred.

- Parenting is the job described in the want-ad. It is the series of tasks necessary to provide food, clothing, shelter, education, and supervision. The performance of this job communicates much that goes beyond the particular task.

- Parenthood is the meaning, value, and experience of a parent. Its nature varies from person to person. It is a matter of ultimate purpose to some, complete indifference to others, and it shapes the quality of parenting.

Parenthood interacting with parenting influences the child in important ways. The significance of this will unfold as the thoughts and feelings of parents are described. You are invited to reflect upon your own experiences as you read. This is an exercise that is likely to reconnect you with feelings that have been lost in the stress of daily living. You may discover that it is refreshing to get back to the basics.

By exploring the irrational elements of decisions to procreate, it becomes clear that parenthood is deeply ingrained in the human psyche. Indeed, a sense of parenthood develops from the moment a neonate encounters his parents. From the preverbal experience, parenthood is shaped and emotional commitment forged. A toddler, grasping his evolutionary nature, demonstrates this by asserting, "When I grow up, I want to be a daddy." So the parenting potential has become a fixed element of personal identity years before the child is capable of rational thinking. At this young age, the essential purpose of existence is recognized and incorporated into the perception of self.

That this is so attests to the power of early parent-child encounters. In the young child's life, the parent—usually the mother—is the infant's very life line. The parent's presence signals nurturance, emotional and physical warmth, excitement, stimulation, and relief from distress. As daily parent-child encounters accrue, a psychological bond with feelings of attachment develops. Such encounters are the prototypic influences of a child's life. Many important perceptions, attitudes, and personal identifications are established. The child senses the self as evolving toward becoming an adult. This understanding is signaled by the child who plays out the fantasy of being a mommy or daddy, an activity that can occupy a child for several years.

A deep and lasting impression of the self as potential parent is a central organizing aspect of key life experiences that follow. Around age five, a child's experiences of family are dominated by fantasies of marrying the opposite sex parent. Resolving this fantasy has a lasting impact on personality development.

Early adolescence signals development of sexual potency and attraction to the opposite sex. Sexual activity is common in Western industrial nations. In the United States, 2000 teenage girls become pregnant every day (significantly higher than that of other industrialized countries). Early sexual activity has become part of the parenting experience. Sexually active teenagers are dealing with the issue of procreation.

Whether casually related, living together, or married, sexually active young adults make the same decisions about procreation as teenagers. Considerations, impulses, and yearnings play into the procreation decision.

———

The experience of one father, Martin, illustrates the depth of the conflicts of parenthood.

> Martin, a thirty-five year old graduate student, had been married for two years to a much younger woman. Despite a promising future, his income was insufficient to support a family. His wife, Marta, who was the primary breadwinner in a stressful, personally unrewarding job,

had traditional expectations of marital roles. Being cast as the main support of the family generated resentment and discontent within her.

The pressure Martin felt, however, came from within himself. His contemporaries, already established in their professions, earned good incomes and enjoyed the comforts of success. Classmates, at least a decade younger, exhibited energy and enthusiasm that were in short supply for him. Martin felt that his position in life alienated him from contemporaries, classmates, and even Marta.

Circumstances required that he continue to plod along. Course work, projects, and training experiences were never ending. He was trapped in a process that had outlived its usefulness, except for the diploma—the ticket to a better life, as remote as ever. He had to persevere. Yet, his view was changing. He no longer sensed life as a languishing trip down a lazy river. Restless and frustrated, it was time to assume control. Yet, he was still in limbo.

During Martin's long bachelorhood, neither bad nor particularly lonely years, he had sensed that family was important to his well-being. Every free-spirited, exciting adventure signaled the call to establish roots. Something was missing and until it was found, life was unsatisfactory, his identity incomplete.

Martin speculated that his feelings derived from a childhood that ended when his mother died. He was twelve years old and with her death, family as he knew it died too. The loss, painful and devastating was softened by his father's determination to maintain the family unit and by the caring response of a large, extended family. Martin developed a deep emotional appreciation of family, and without it his adult life was neither complete nor secure.

These powerful urges were strong enough to overcome the sense that he could not start his own family.

Consider Martin's struggle with the decision to become a parent. His readiness for parenthood is a good point of departure. Many people express doubts about being ready. Ideally, we resolve our own growing-up issues, establish ourselves socially and professionally, and then enter into a marriage made in heaven. Accomplishing all these milestones by early adulthood, we then begin our family. Without job or adequate financial resources, Martin was clearly unready by these standards. Dependence upon his wife as breadwinner created tension in his marriage. Martin was responding to his own internal imperatives—a sense that he was growing old before he had finished growing up.

I have heard many interpretations of readiness. One father believed it was instinctive, that he would sense when the time was right. To him, nature determined when one was ready. Others talked about personal or marital milestones. One couple felt the decision to procreate arose from a sense of growth in their relationship. It was a shared adventure that developed new vistas for love and caring. Another couple expressed the same idea in more mundane terms: it was time to do more in the relationship than go to the movies. Still others take the decision for granted. The motive is sex, not procreation and what will be, will be.

The pull of family experience was overriding for Martin. The many strands of the force directing that pull included his mother's death, the rescue of his extended family, and his sense of incompleteness. Early socialization had instilled a sense of family as the natural context of life.

These lessons exert so powerful an influence that to choose not to replicate in adulthood what was learned as a child requires determination to overcome them. In fact, some seek to establish correspondence between childhood and adulthood. One father felt a strong urge to have a second child because he had been raised in a two child family. All other considerations—finances, likelihood of a difficult second pregnancy, and his own personal ambition—carried little weight in the decision. He needed a two child family to feel right.

The link between past and present may be less florid in other cases, but inevitably it is a factor.

Sandi, a mother of two small daughters, tenderly reminisced about her own childhood. These fond memories impelled her to pass similar experiences on to succeeding generations. Interestingly, her husband, Hal, had strong urges to be a father to compensate for what was missing in his childhood. From opposite sides of the coin, Sandi and Hal required children as a means for expressing urges that had originated in their pasts.

Samantha, mother of a young son, felt she had been emotionally damaged by her own mother and needed to prove she could be a decent parent. For her, parenting provided the test of whether she had overcome the damage.

For some, ties to the past are genetic as well as psychological. For them, a sense of biological continuity is meaningful. When asked to speculate about an adoptive child, for example, many believe their responses would be different than to a birth child. There is a perception that blood intensifies the relationship.

Maury, an orthodox Jewish father of an adoptive son traced his familial roots to a priestly tribe that enjoyed special privileges and obligations. An involved and caring parent, it troubled Maury that his son entered a special sanctuary reserved for direct descendants of the priestly tribe. Maury felt that his son had violated the sanctuary because he lacked the genetic criteria. His own ambivalence about the adoption was highlighted by this reaction.

Genetic continuity to the past and into the future, was lacking for Maury. For many, it is a primary motive for having a child. Birth ties everyone to the origins of life on earth. Without the extension of continuity through offspring, death assigns us to oblivion. To preserve the family line, some men feel obligated to leave sons to carry on the family name and genes.

Others respond to the urge to perpetuate their sense of connection. This expresses a tribal or racial feeling of a personal obligation to preserve their cultural, genetic group. The biblical story of Isaac directly relates to this issue. Isaac contributed little to the development of the nation of Israel. Yet, had he not had sons and passed on to them knowledge of the God of Abraham, the nation would have ceased to exist. Merely creating children and passing along the tradition enabled Isaac to play an important role in the continuity of his people. The story of Isaac captures the feelings reported by many modern parents. It can be a powerful motive for procreation.

The previous stories covered some of the reasons why people may choose to become parents.

 ✦ Reliving and/or undoing the past,

- Personal fulfillment and identity enhancement,

- Cementing or restoring a marital relationship,

- Projecting spiritual and material self into the future to continue family or tribal lines and to remain immortal.

The list hardly scratches the surface. Many children are conceived for no apparent reason. They are products of impulsive, casual sexual liaisons. Conception is like Russian roulette—a game of chance. In one study of unwed teenage females, only nineteen percent of those who had not intended to become pregnant had used birth control consistently. Other studies confirm that a vast majority of sexually active adolescent teenagers ignore birth control, consciously or unconsciously risking pregnancy. Among the reasons for resulting pregnancies were loneliness, replacement of personal loss, compensating for prior abortion, anger toward parents/authority figures, attention seeking, immature behavior, and pressuring a boyfriend into marriage. Some boyfriends wanted the child, supposedly to enhance their masculinity or because of peer or sibling role modeling.

These were studies of lower socioeconomic groups and caution should be used against overgeneralizing the results. But clinical experience suggests that such factors do influence procreative decisions across socioeconomic and age lines. A middle-class couple who felt themselves drifting apart from friends with children and felt they needed a child to continue the friendships. One father half jokingly said that he became a father, "because my mother would kill me if I didn't." Other middle class people report pregnancies related to past miscarriages, other losses, or to shore up foundering relationships.

Such irrational reasons are the wrong incentives for having a child. Conception cannot resolve personal problems and will only create a host of additional problems. The demands of parenting can be so overwhelming that both the new baby and the parents are damaged in the process.

Do any rational elements contribute to the decision to bear a child? While not all irrationality is bad, it would be comforting to find at least a bit of rationality in the process. The preceding examples describe primal, neurotic, and idealistic reasons for procreation expressing nothing of our sensible, humanistic side. We can assume that rational factors are involved. Yet, people do not readily report that such factors bear upon the decision to procreate. Perhaps they are so obvious that they are taken for granted. There are no better reasons for procreation than the joy in having a child, satisfaction of influencing his development, parental pride, finding love between child and parent, and the fun of interacting in a continuous, long-term relationship. No other motives can compensate for the absence of these.

Figure 1.1 summarizes the major influences on the decision to procreate. It illustrates the complexity of the decision and emphasizes the extent to which irrationality contributes to it.

Creating a child requires no creativity, only sexual coupling and chance which are within the range of virtually all humanity. But raising that child requires commitment, perseverance, tolerance, and creative responses. This baffling irony poses a tremendous dilemma in the modern world. The most important task in life can be thrust upon the least equipped, least prepared. Rather than a blessing, it is more sensible to attribute this irony to a god with a rather wicked sense of humor. The failure of individuals and society to deal with the important consequences of parenthood is appallingly obvious.

Figure 1.1   Motivations For Procreating

Level V	Noble-Rational
	Love of Children
	Joy in Parenthood
	Meaning and Fulfillment in Life
Level IV	Noble-Irrational
	Immortality
	Preservation of Family Name
	Religious or National Imperative
	Undo or Relive the Past
Level III	Neurotic
	Solve a Personal Problem
	Loneliness
Level II	Interpersonal Manipulation
	Control of a Relationship
	Expression of Hostility
	Maintain Dependency
Level I	Primal
	Irresponsible Sex

Understanding motivation—at best a very mixed bag—
begins the process of wrestling with parenthood. Should
this bag contain insufficient amounts of love, joy, and
pride of parenthood, what will sustain a parent over the
long haul—the long, cranky nights, the terrible twos, the
inevitable rebellions, petty squabbles, the pain of emancipation, endless crises, triumphs and failures? Without
deeper meaning, parenting can deteriorate into neglect
and indifference and even abuse. Living through these
complex trials has nothing to do with immortality, undoing the past, proving sexuality, or compensating for loss.
Even blessed events are fleeting. But, to sustain over the
long haul, some noble elements should be included when
choosing to have children.

Many parents run into difficulty along the way. Myriad issues that thwart or spoil the parent-child relationship will
arise. There is no magical formula. Sensitivity to the issue
of motivation is vital as it shapes the nature of the parent-
child encounter. To be sure, it is one of several factors,
but it is the most basic. Technique, discipline, and communication are not the essence of the problem. A parent
must understand, then accept the basic reasons for bringing this child into the world. This understanding can re-
generate a positive relationship with the child. It is worth
repeating: without the love, joy, and pride of parenthood,
parenting is reduced to child care or worse—abuse.

Parenthood is not a job but a state of mind. It is about
meaning, values, emotional qualities, and commitment.
Next we'll focus on the characteristics that set parenthood
apart from parenting and make it the most important consideration in a decision to have children.

Chapter 2

Commitments—Ego and Time

What I really would have preferred was to remain a writer who dabbled in motherhood. . . . But Molly would not permit it. She needed a mother, not a dabbler.
Erica Jong, *Fear of Fifty*, 1994

Without a strong sense of parenthood, the job of parenting offers little reward. Joyous acts of love are reduced to menial tasks and grudging obligation. Parenting without parenthood is nothing more than child care and communicates neither love nor a sense of speciality or security. Parenthood is the quality that communicates and assigns value and importance to a child. It requires a dedicated commitment of ego and time.

A couple of three year olds are playing in a pool. The little girl, Susan, paddles quietly, timidly. She isn't having a good time. The little boy, Stephen, is fully engaged. His exuberance is contagious. The children are close but don't interact. Their fathers sit by the pool talking. The boy elicits his father's attention and involvement. His father is responsive, a cheer leader who flips coins for his son to re-

15

trieve. Soon, he too is in the pool, tossing Stephen in the air and towing him around. Susan watches closely then feebly attempts to engage her father. He is passive and indifferent. Susan resumes her joyless play. Two children have spent an hour at the pool with daddy. How different is that hour. Susan experienced parenting without parenthood. Stephen had it all.

Ego

Parenthood implies that being a parent is high on one's personal agenda and that a substantial portion of ego is invested in the role. The act of raising a child is fulfilling and a source of gratification. The classic "Jewish" mother is so totally invested that her existence is valid only in her capacity to mother. To let go of her children threatens her sense of self. The opposite extreme is represented by a person who finds little fulfillment in the image of self as parent, resulting in indifference to the child. Little pride, gratification, and meaningfulness evolve for that parent resulting in harm to the child's welfare.

Most of us have diverse ego investments, and parenthood is only one aspect of our identity. Some are invested in professions. Worth is measured by success at work. Pride in accomplishment assumes great importance. Ego is on the line as the career ladder is ascended. Almost any aspect of human experience can command a degree of ego investment. Nationality, athletic ability, and the sense of self as lover or comic can be used to build a self-image and are expressed by one's decisions and actions. One who takes great pride in the image of self as golfer spends much time golfing. A Casanova invests in the pursuit and conquest of women.

Such ego commitments compete with each other and capture varying amounts of ego. The "Jewish" mother, the careerist, and the Casanova illustrate that implicit internal hierarchies determine one's direction. An internal agenda directs one to decide what is more important. Parenthood may be important but how important compared to other areas of investment? Unless it is relatively high on the personal agenda, it is swept aside by other areas of ego investment.

A tale of two doctors—each divorced, each believing that a custodial mother is an inadequate parent— illustrates differing values of parenthood.

Dr. Peters, a deeply religious man who professed a strong commitment to family, made a heroic effort to preserve a very troubled marriage. Despite those efforts, his wife filed for divorce and gained custody of their two young children. Dr. Peters viewed his ex-wife as morally and emotionally unfit as a parent. He felt that her parenting would irrevocably damage their children. Without his strong presence in his children's lives, he feared they would develop serious problems. Notwithstanding his strong parenthood values, Dr. Peters remarried and accepted a position out of state. He now communicates with his children by phone every week, and they spend two lengthy visitations together each year.

Dr. Franklin had a thriving practice in the east. His ex-wife, the custodial parent, moved out of state. Telephoning his young children, Dr. Franklin was alarmed by what they told him. He concluded that they were neglected and subjected to harmful influences. Dr. Franklin closed his practice and relocated to the city where his children lived. He established a new practice and remained until his children graduated from high school and established

independence. He, too, has remarried. He accomplished
what Dr. Peters had but without abandoning his children.

The example of the two doctors shows that while parenthood may be a deeply held conviction, it competes with
other areas of life experience. For Dr. Peters, career and remarriage took precedence over parenthood. For Dr. Franklin, parenthood came first. Practical decisions are
influenced by the ego investments we make. And while
the stakes may not be as high as those of Drs. Peters and
Franklin, we all have dilemmas to resolve. Should we attend a professional meeting or spend the evening at
home? Should the children go on the vacation or be left
with a babysitter? These are not necessarily dramatic decisions to make, but the cumulative weight of our day-to-
day choices has significant impact. Without a strong
sense of parenthood, children's needs will be underesti-
mated.

Time

Not only ego is invested, but also time. We lead busy lives
with seldom enough time to take care of everything. Each
hour is like a block from which we construct our lives.
The arrangement of these blocks reveals much about our
priorities and values—what we believe and who we are.
Time allotment is the ultimate existential bottom line.
Each hour committed to one or another endeavor elimi-
nates that hour from other uses. Degrees of freedom are
lost with each choice of how to use our time.

We aren't totally free to arrange these time blocks. Time is
tightly structured, and freedom is lost just by attending
to basic physiological needs. Sleep and other bedroom activities—intimacy, reading, or listening to talk-radio—

consume approximately seven hours daily or forty-nine of our total 168 hours available each week as shown in Figure 2.1. It hardly seems fair. A mere 119 hours remain for waking activities.

More time is used to gratify other basic needs. Eating, bathing, and toilet activities take about twenty-one hours each week. Another ten hours are spent cooking, shopping, washing dishes and clothes, maintaining the household and car, throwing out the garbage, doing yard work, and paying bills. Simple recreational activities, watching television, reading, or working a jigsaw puzzle, consume fifteen hours per week. There are only seventy-three hours left.

Basic economic survival normally depends on a traditional forty hour a week job with an additional ten hours

Figure 2.1   Weekly Time Accounting Sheet

Category	Est. Hours	% of Time	Actual Hours	% of Time
Sleep	49	29.0	_____	____
Need Satisfaction	21	12.5	_____	____
Domestic Chores	11	6.5	_____	____
Relaxation	15	9.0	_____	____
Employment	50	30.0	_____	____
Social/Spousal	12	7.0	_____	____
Hobbies	10	6.0	_____	____
TOTAL	168	100.0	_____	____
Remaining Time For Parenting	0	0.0	_____	____

preparing for work and commuting. Amazingly, we are left with twenty-three discretionary hours each week, less than one full day to live our lives. The other one hundred forty-five hours have been devoted to survival.

Social activities with a church group, political party, volunteer work, and communication with friends and relatives may take up to five hours per week. Private time spent with a spouse dining out, going for walks, visiting the local coffee bar or ice cream parlor—another seven hours gone.

All work and no play makes Jack a dull boy and Jill a dull girl. Golf, softball, bowling, jogging, biking, aerobics, and pumping iron take a lot of time. It is not unusual to devote about ten hours per week to these activities.

We have accounted for the 168 hours in the week. Granting variations or unusual circumstances most lives roughly fit the example. No time was squandered. No time was committed to parenting.

Time resources are depleted by attending to necessities. Are we any better off than the giant denizens of the deep who spend their lives roaming and scavenging for sufficient nourishment to sustain their bulk? No time exists for higher level pursuits: cavorting with the muses, contemplating the meaning of life, raising a child. When is there time to write the great American novel, to train for a marathon, to master the five string banjo, learn about the kings of England, or to enjoy the miracle of a growing child?

How does parenting fit into the lives of average, well-meaning people? How does it fit into the lives of the selfish, the disturbed, and those driven by passion or ambition? How does it fit into the lives of those who have children for dubious reasons? Parenting presents enormous problems for any parent, especially those whose personal agenda and role gratification are compromised by raising children. These problems are magnified in the ever increasing pool of single parents with more responsibilities in their 168 hours per week than the average two parent family.

Annette exemplifies a single parent who struggles with her own needs and those of her children.

Annette was thirty-five year old who divorced the alcoholic father of her fifteen year old daughter and seven year old son. She married at seventeen to escape the oppression of an unhappy home life and slipped into the depressing role of the wife of an alcoholic. Annette missed the experience of emancipation and independence that would have enabled her to mature and develop a sense of self. Parenting was thrust upon her before she completed growing up.

After her divorce, she obtained a job in retailing and was placed in the company's management training program. Learning the new job and training for a management position required more than a forty hour work week. In addition to her involvement in AL-ANON, an organization for families of alcoholics, she became socially active again.

There was nothing inherently unreasonable, inappropriate, or selfish in what she was doing, but responsibilities to her children called for a somewhat different allocation. Her son developed behavioral problems and was placed in therapy. He was an angry, destructive child who functioned only marginally in school. The message was clear—he assumed a position that was too low on his mother's priority list. He needed more from her than she was giving. Annette was aware of the dilemma, but could not be the parent her son and daughter needed unless she changed the personal agenda that emphasized her job and active social life.

Annette resolved to settle into a position lower than management level and to reduce her social activities. This allowed her to spend more time with her children and attend to their needs. Eventually she met and married a loving, caring man and returned to the role of homemaker.

It was not easy for Annette to change for the sake of her children. However, once her son's distress was heeded she did make positive parenting decisions.

Rita, a thirty year old, handsome divorcee, had married in her teens and became the mother of a son and two daughters. Her blue-collar husband held conventional views of a wife's role. He discouraged her attempt to take courses and meet interesting people. Rita felt stifled and controlled and eventually divorced him.

She then entered college and became an outstanding student. She supported her family by working in a medical school laboratory. Her mentors were impressed with her abilities and encouraged her to pursue a medical degree. Rita also began a relationship with another student. Student, laboratory assistant, paramour, and parent—her life was full.

The children's emotional needs suffered not only from lack of their mother's attention but from the effective abandonment of their father, who was embittered and hurt by the divorce. Rita gave what she could but it was not enough. The needy children became angry and destructive. Their unhappiness was apparent, and only the youngest functioned close to her potential in school.

They were paying the price for their mother's academic and social pursuits.

Rita realized that her agenda was not working for her children and decided that adjustments were needed. She was unwilling to sacrifice her children's emotional health for a medical degree. She earned a bachelor's degree with honors and accepted challenging work in a genetics laboratory. The quest for a higher degree was postponed until her children were older. It was enough to settle for half a loaf now and feel that she was coming through for her children.

Again, it's apparent that changes in time allotments can improve the parenting dilemma, but it is not easy. For both Annette and Rita needed to slow down, postpone ambition, and reorder their lives to be more available to their children. They could do so only if parenthood values ranked high on the personal agenda. Obviously, they did.

Many two-parent families also have difficulty in allocating time to parenting.

A law student mother and airline pilot father placed their only child, Danny, with babysitters and preschools before he was two years old so they could pursue careers. He was in good hands and happy. As caring and loving parents, they enjoyed the time spent with their son. But by second grade, Danny was in trouble. He had become a passive-aggressive child who did not function well in school. It was this behavior that got his parents involved.

Constructing a balanced life with room for personal fulfillment, marital and social gratification, career development and effective parenting is an impossible project for many. Something has to give or someone will pay the price. A parent who sacrifices career or social life to fulfill parenting obligations inevitably resents the burden. A neglected child will react in emotionally arresting and self-defeating ways. It isn't right or wrong. Right is on every side of the issue. It is simply a human dilemma.

Those who need to make a mark upon the world, experience delayed adolescence, enjoy a full social life, or scale the career ladder may have insufficient time to raise their children. Many children suffer as a result. Suffering does not imply that children are irrevocably damaged in the process, but neither should it be minimized or discounted. Some suffering is unavoidable. How, then, can the problems of Annette, Rita, and others be avoided?

A note of painful realism: To some degree, the problem is not solvable. Competition between needs and agendas is inevitable, and it is unrealistic to expect that conflicting schedules will always be resolved in favor of the children. The scarce resource of the parent's time must be distributed in the most equitable and workable way.

A partial solution is to critically appraise how our time is spent and that is what Figure 2.1 helps us to do. If your family comes first, but you spend large chunks of time at the bowling alley, in committee meetings, or at the local bar, analyze this discrepancy. While many hours in the week are set, others are discretionary. Choices can be made. The trap is a lack of understanding that we can choose to do it differently and do the right thing for our children.

There is no time without choosing to make time. We choose from a pool of competing needs. No choice is made without cost. To attend to the needs of one's child is to choose not to spend the evening with the boys, work overtime, or chair a meeting. Unless strongly invested in the role of parent, children's needs are minimized and even ignored. Parents may believe their child can do without them. They will underestimate the child's needs and misjudge how well he is functioning.

———

Ego investment in parenting provides contentment and completion, confirms that parenting complements rather than competes with the personal agenda, and insures pride and gratification in raising a child. Clearly, young parents, those starting over, and those with strong personal aspirations have difficulty investing their egos sufficiently in parenting. Without the investment of ego, no adequate commitment of time is possible.

Time commitments often seem unrelated to choice, and life emerges in response to necessity and factors beyond our control. This observation is valid only if our ability and will to construct life differently is ignored.

The process of gaining control is simple to explain but sometimes difficult to achieve. It begins with the assessment of who in the family is paying the price for what. The place to begin the assessment is the behavior and emotionality of the children. If dysfunction or unhappiness is detected, parents should know that something, not necessarily parental time, is not working for the child. For example, a poor athlete or learning disabled child may be teased and rejected. Life away from home is misery. To resolve those issues may not entail rethinking parental priorities. But if parents appraise how their time is allocated, they may discover a pattern that leaves too little time for parenting. We can adjust our priorities, but only if there is an ego payoff. To sacrifice for the kids leads to resentment. Pro-parenting choices call for readjusting the agenda.

In the previous story of Annette, she made the choice to give up some of her outside activities and increase the time spent with her children. Putting responsibility of her young son first was truly a positive parenthood decision

_____

Parenting demands time, money, and emotional involvement. Be wary of sentimental pap about the wonders and joys of parenting. It is hard, often unrewarding work to raise a child. Unless you are ready to have a child, parenting will negatively affect you and the child. Yet, no matter how carefully you plan, circumstances may impel adjustment as you move through the stages of life.

> Margaret, in her early thirties, is unmarried, and chronically depressed. Because she distrusts relationships, even non-romantic ones, she has not found happiness with men.
>
> Margaret is bright and competent, but she hates her job and resents her father for discouraging her artistic inclinations in high school. She is emotionally suppressed and terribly alone. Frightened and insecure, she is inwardly relieved when terminated from her job. This provides her with an excuse to go to art school.
>
> A year after Margaret became an art student, a brief romantic involvement ended. Although she was pregnant, she wanted nothing to do with her former lover.
>
> Years earlier, her doctor had told her that she was infertile. Obviously, she was quite unprepared to be a birth parent. Margaret dropped out of school but planned to return after having the baby.

Although Margaret ignored the father, did the child have the right to know and relate to him? Of course.

Margaret had to reallocate her time and readjust her personal agenda. She fought the urge to throw in the towel. But resigning from the job of parent isn't an option, regardless of satisfaction. If inclined toward introspection, perhaps after a three a.m. feeding, Margaret will ponder about where it all leads. She may feel a commitment and attachment to her baby and question what she can do for her. What is her purpose?

The issue of raising of a child will loom large for Margaret. Her ego investment in being a parent is slight. Until her pregnancy, parenthood had little relevance to her quest for fulfillment and happiness. Her ego was invested in developing herself as artist. But circumstances created a dilemma. If Margaret cannot redirect ego to parenthood, her lifelong sense of being discouraged from artistic expression will be shifted to her baby. The time spent in raising her child will be compromised without an ego investment in parenthood.

_____

Figure 2.2 can help in assessing whether adequate ego and time are invested in parenting. Being critically honest is important in placing oneself in the proper quadrant of the figure. A plus (+) indicates an adequate to ample amount of ego or time investment. A minus (-) indicates inadequate to no ego or time involvement in parenting.

Quadrant I
This is the most favorable of the quadrants if not overdone. Adequate ego and time are invested.

Quadrant II
Adequate ego but inadequate time is invested in child

Figure 2.2.   Parenthood Quadrants

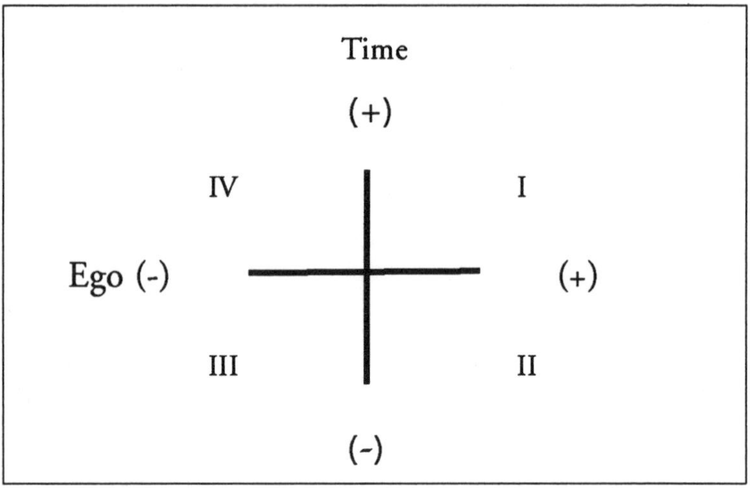

```
                    Time
                    (+)

         IV          |          I
                     |
Ego (-)  ———————————+———————————  (+)
                     |
         III         |          II

                    (-)
```

rearing. This may be a well meaning parent who does not fully realize the needs of the child until a problem arises.

Quadrant III
With inadequate ego and time this is the most problematic quadrant. This is the least favorable situation for children and unless changed, will likely lead to psychological growth problems.

Quadrant IV
Adequate time but little ego involvement. Time may be spent passively watching television with the children or shuttling them from one activity to another. Parents may be physically present and give adequate supervision, but positive emotional involvement is lacking.

Investment of ego and time increases the probability for wholesome, psychological growth of children. If neither is invested, the child's future is bleak and will likely lead to behavioral and emotional problems. It is difficult for these children to develop a sense of being valued, feeling special and appreciated, and commitment to and from adults. Depression, rejection of adult values, and affiliation with those who feel similarly are clinical expressions in children deprived of parental investment.

A strong ego commitment to parenthood that is unmatched by an adequate time commitment leads children to feelings of betrayal and distrust. Adults are viewed as hypocritical and untrustworthy. Such children develop misgivings about relationships and become cautious about investing themselves in others.

The investment of time without a corresponding commitment of ego leads to perfunctory parenting. No matter how well the physical needs are addressed, the emotional needs of the child are wanting. Depression, feelings of ineffectualness, and passivity can result.

Place yourself in the quadrant that best represents your situation. If that is not where you want to be, you now have an opportunity to adjust what needs attention. You are now wrestling with parenthood!

Chapter 3

The Good Parent

Scientists have been unable to discover many profound principles that relate the action of mothers, fathers, or siblings to psychological characteristic in the child.
Jerome Kagan, *The Nature of the Child*, 1984

Time and ego commitments of parents are a good beginning for children. They are necessary but not sufficient to raise a child. For the manner in which parenting is performed has a crucial impact on children. It is not only *what* we do, but *how* we do it that matters. Temperament determines how it will be done.

Temperament describes emotional tendencies, the components of all action and reaction. This essential nature of ourselves defines us to others. It is particularly true that infants and young children define parents by their temperaments. To them, it matters not if we are rich, famous, or exceptionally brilliant. Our interests, political views, or hobbies are irrelevant. Children have no idea how beautiful we are or if our clothes are color coordinated. But they respond to our moods and emotional reactions. In-

31

deed, our children know us first by our temperamental qualities. They know if we are warm, relaxed, accepting, even tempered, or playful. Children are keenly responsive to numerous, subtle temperamental qualities. From the time of their birth, infants begin learning about feelings. This knowledge tells them a lot about the world in which they live and about who they are. No other knowledge is more important to them.

Obviously, there is a wide range of personality types that include a variety of temperamental qualities. Some are with us from birth and endure a lifetime. We are born with certain response tendencies—to be mellow, fussy, responsive, and so on—which are modulated or exaggerated by experience. By adulthood, our temperamental qualities are virtually fixed.

Some of these tendencies may be compatible with the demands of parenting, others may not. Most would agree that it is better to be warm, nurturing, and calm than angry, cold, or indifferent. Patience is a virtue, irritability a detriment. Few parents, if any, possess only wholesome temperamental qualities. What we do about our negative temperamental nature illustrates the kind of parent we are.

The very nature of child rearing magnifies the impact of temperament. Parenting makes intense emotional demands. It is a job we cannot responsibly quit. That the primary work place is also one's home compounds the difficulty. Paradoxically, home is a sanctuary for some. But it is also a work place that commands attention to someone else's needs. One's retreat from stress may generate stresses of its own. These can arouse the worst tendencies and overwhelm our best intentions.

Temperamental qualities determine the way in which issues are addressed. Often, the manner of transmission is more important than the issue, for it communicates lessons that are basic, durable, and quite salient. A lasting impact can shape a child's world view or self-concept. A demanding, critical father communicates feelings of disappointment and perhaps anger. The son feels he cannot please his father or measure up to his standards. Such experience tends to generalize and create feelings of inadequacy. Surely, no well-meaning father would want to communicate such feelings.

Temperamental qualities determine the home's emotional climate and creates either a happy home or one that is tense, threatening, and uncomfortable. At the extreme, an abusive atmosphere may result. If that occurs, the emotional climate cannot sustain wholesome psychological growth. Any influence of existing, positive qualities is canceled in an abusive atmosphere.

> A deeply religious, involved, and loving father assumed responsibility for his son's socialization and moral development. His demands were unrealistic. His tolerance was entirely lacking, and nurturance evolved into forced feeding. Toilet training was coercive. The child was manhandled, thrown into chairs. Temperamentally unsuited to parent, this father had damaged his son.

Most parents to one degree or another wrestle with temperamental qualities and unresolved conflicts inherited from their pasts. None of us is so pure in heart, in control of the inner self, mature, and on top of things as to always react in growth enhancing ways. Frequently, tempers are short, we lack patience, and our own needs come first. We are brusque, say things we don't mean, and react unfairly. Sometimes we are unduly intrusive, overprotective, and unfair. For before we are parents, we are human beings with strengths and weaknesses.

We are not obligated to be perfect, but we should learn to know ourselves. We should not indulge in self-deception or rationalize our flaws and ignore the need to control tendencies that adversely affect our children. Upon hearing that alcohol damages fetuses or smoking endangers an asthmatic child, the responsible parent inhibits such behaviors. So, too, will that parent change other tendencies that damage children. If we accept our behavior without changing harmful tendencies, we shortchange our children and demean ourselves as parents.

The capacity to examine one's reactions and to effect solutions to detrimental patterns is vitally important to responsible child rearing. Myriad tasks and challenges also must be mastered, from child development to nutrition, availability of community resources, discipline, and changing diapers. Dozens of self-help books, parenting classes, and mentors (such as grandparents) can assist parents in acquiring good parenting skills and knowledge to the benefit of both child and parent.

But, where is this leading? We influence our children, provide guidance and hope to instill values. We know what kind of person we want our child to be. Although our awareness may be vague and unarticulated, we envision goals to accomplish. What are these goals? How can we direct our parenting efforts and evaluate how well we are doing?

Typically, we rely on instinct and respond to daily challenges as they occur. If our parenthood values are sufficient, we experience pleasure and meaning through our efforts.

Life is more complex than in the past. Our children question or reject our values. They exhibit offensive characteristics. It is important to understand what actions we, as parents, are taking which contribute to our children's negative behaviors. We often react emotionally in ways that undermine us as parents. Then caught up in disappointment we lose track of our goals.

Mary, a widow with three adolescent sons, was perturbed by her youngest child. Mark was almost sixteen. For the family to function smoothly, he needed to be responsible and self-sufficient. Mark had serious learning disabilities and problems functioning in school. He found learning to be highly unrewarding. But he was socially adept, and school provided him good opportunities to socialize. Mark valued play and being with his friends. He aspired to play professional basketball, despite his lack of success in the sport. He had difficulty waking up in the morning, came home late at night, spent only a few minutes a night studying. He was close to flunking out of school.

Mary embarked on a course to rescue Mark from himself. She awakened him in the morning and imposed strict consequences when he came home late. She provided a tutor, intervened with the school so he wouldn't be expelled, and monitored his homework. She protected him from failure.

But did Mary enhance Mark's feelings of responsibility and self-sufficiency? One can easily empathize with Mary. Her son challenged her beyond reason. She remained patient and supportive due to her strong parenthood values. Time was a problem because of the demands of her job, but she certainly was available to the extent possible. Her problem was losing sight of the ultimate goal. Mark could not develop responsibility while his mother continued to rescue him from the consequences of his behavior. Upon realizing this, Mary had little difficulty giving Mark back the responsibility for his own life. She needed to accept that Mark would have to deal with the consequences of his actions. How could he learn to be responsible when she took responsibility for him? Perhaps Mark will grow into responsibility as he matures.

What can a parent do? We will save the answer for the next section.

———

The late anthropologist, Margaret Mead, believed that in rapidly changing times it is difficult for parents to know what lessons to teach their children. Today's parents don't know what kind of world awaits their children, nor what skills, attitudes, and characteristics will be valuable. Parents have become less and less influential. Surrogates, the media, and kids on the street influence a child's life more than parents. Given this, what are the goals of parenting?

Parenting Goals

Traditionally, children have been reflections of their parenting. The wayward, troubled, socially rude, or spoiled child reflects poorly on his parents. Subtly or overtly, parents are held accountable, blamed, even scorned by teachers, physicians, and neighbors for their child's misdeeds. Open condemnation is likely to be aimed toward the parent who abuses, neglects, or fails to provide an environment of safety and shelter. Even a child with minor emotional or behavioral difficulties raises eyebrows vis-à-vis the parent.

At the other end of the line is the child who functions well, the popular child with the right friends who excels in school and is involved in appropriate activities. Such a child is viewed as a credit to parents who must be doing something right. For some, a socially acceptable child is a sign of successful parenting.

But many maintain that social approval is not the end goal of parenting. For them, how the child feels about himself is more relevant. Sigmund Freud believed that a child secure in the love of his mother has no fear of failure as an adult. Providing this and other positive feelings about the self is viewed as a deeper, more meaningful goal of parenting. How others view the child or rate the quality of parenting is secondary, and the child probably views reactions and judgment of others as irrelevant.

To be remembered fondly, verifies the success of the parent-child relationship. This goal is more modest. Many parents are satisfied to give to their child in ways to be remembered with kindness, to provide values he can draw upon to cope with inevitable stresses and trials. These parents implicitly believe that children grow in their own way, rather than fit parental models.

To have the child follow in a parent's footsteps is an important goal for others. A child born into a deeply religious family is acculturated to adopt the style, mores, and beliefs of his religious community. The process by which this is done can profoundly affect the child in all aspects of his personal and interpersonal experience. In such a cultural atmosphere, the success of parenting can be ascertained by the degree to which the child accepts the values.

The issue need not be religious. The child may be expected to follow the parent in matters such as education or business. The book, *Giant*, described a father's rejection of his son who chose to be a physician rather than a rancher. To many, it seems silly for a father to consider himself a failure because his son became a doctor. But the underlying issue was not one of profession per se. The real issue was the father's rigid view of manliness; rugged, aggressive, and hard. In the father's eyes, the choice to become a physician was unmanly and clearly a failure in parenting.

Not all parenting goals are cast far into the future. The parent's encounter with the child is immediate and daily. To enjoy them is the essence of parenting. Such experiences usually occur when the child is happy and content, willingly goes along with the parent, and does well in the physical, emotional, and social spheres.

These parenting goals are not mutually exclusive. Some may be emphasized more than others, but they describe what parents generally want for their children.

Simply put, the ultimate goal of parenting is to help the child grow up. We all know that the psychology of the newly born is different from that of the mature adult. Differences are found in emotion, thought, learning, perception, and motivation. Life is a progression along developmental roads, and the parent is the most important tour guide for the child. The goal is not always clear. There is nothing inevitable about growing up. Many people fail to progress very far along the developmental road. Anna Freud, the late child psychoanalyst, described the process in more cogent terms. She defined personality development as "the child's capacity to move forward in progressive steps until maturation, development in all areas of the personality, and adaptation to the social community have been completed."*

The good parent is a positive influence in this process. The goal is to create physical and psychological conditions that enable the child to move forward, to recognize the progressive steps to maturation, and to facilitate adaptation to the social community. These parameters of parenting include a host of qualities, more than any one of us possesses. But, no matter, we have been recruited for the job.

Time, roles, parental goals, and personal qualities establish the dimensions of parenting. Competition among needs, obligations, commitments, and desires is great. The discrepancy between parenting goals and parenting commitments also may be great. Confusion and conflict in the lives of parents and their children make it difficult to determine what good parenting is all about.

Establishing goals is relatively easy. Achieving them is the demanding part of the job. Offspring are seldom compliant; they are subject to influences beyond parental control; the style of parenting may clash with the temperament of the child, leading to conflict and rejection of parental values. Unwittingly, the wrong lessons may be communicated to the child. Even the nature of parenting changed not long ago.

Changes in Parenting

The job and aims of parenting once were easy to define. Parenting was a full-time job in a field dominated by females with responsibility of primary care of the children. Mothers shaped the view acquired by the child. The father's role was secondary in that it was one of several a

*Freud, Anna, *Normality and Pathology in Childhood: Assessments of Development*, (New York: International Universities Press, Inc., 1965), 123.

man assumed. Fathering was a part-time job, after a full day's work. The father served as the ultimate authority or disciplinarian, decision maker, mentor, and symbol of life away from the family scene. He influenced the child's sense of justice, confidence, and development of dreams and ideas.

The contemporary situation is complicated by a world of dual breadwinners, single parents, and latchkey kids. Emancipated adults may find insufficient ego gratification in the parental role. It is devalued in our society.

Parenting is no longer a full-time job. In many cases, its functions are not direct care. For many men and women, the primary sources of ego gratification are career, developing personal talents, and acquiring symbols of success and power. Regardless of station in life, it generally requires two wage earners to adequately support a family. The job of parenting must be approached in new ways.

Rather than hands-on operational, parenting has evolved into a position of administration. The good mother no longer keeps the children clean, gets them off to school on time, and leisurely spends a couple of hours baking an apple pie. Today she arranges the best babysitter and after school care. She seeks out the best enrichment programs and is the most creative in designing a summer program to keep the children safe, entertained, and busy. Many functions directly assumed by parents in the past are farmed out to surrogates. This is a widespread American phenomenon.

With all these forces at work, it is easy to lose sight of goals or to establish goals which are impossible to attain, to feel overwhelmed, or focus on irrelevant issues. Thousands of things can go wrong. It is urgent that we keep matters in perspective. I propose that this can be done simply by delineating the tasks and issues that affect child rearing including parenthood, parenting, and parental temperament. Specifying the diverse aspects of child rearing decreases the problem's magnitude and renders the course more manageable. A profile of strengths and weaknesses can be created. A simple formula, derived from the athletic world can be applied. To become a champion, work on weaknesses until they become strengths. By applying this formula to child rearing, parents can improve their parenting tools.

Parent Report Card

What could be simpler than a Parent Report Card (see Figure 3.1)? I invite parents to rate themselves in all the categories. Don't be modest. Praise yourself for good performance. You deserve to be good to yourself. But also admit your weaknesses. As you identify deficits, you reveal opportunities to correct the problem. Indeed, perfect parenting doesn't exist, and even if it did, it would be detrimental to your child's development. Honest appraisal is the beginning of wisdom. You owe it to yourself as well as to your child.

To analyze the interaction of parenting elements, I have divided parenting into three major categories: job skills, parenting role, and temperament. For each category the main elements are listed.

Job Skills

The job skills of parenting include the most basic elements. Parents who get high marks in this area furnish basic material items such as food, clothing, and shelter. They are sensitive toward the child, allowing them to de-

Figure 3.1   Parent Report Card

	Child's Age		
	0-5	6-12	13-18
JOB SKILLS			
Child Care			
Behavior Management			
Enrichment			
Communication			
Knowledge and Expectations			
Goals			
Flexibility			
ROLE			
Emotional Investment			
Time Commitment			
Joy and Satisfaction			
Role Model			
Emotional Accessibility			
Identification			
TEMPERAMENT			
Emotional Climate			
Patience			
Sensitivity to Child's Need			
Control Maintenance and Relinquishment			
Perspective			
Crisis Management			
Control of Self			

Grade Points

A = Outstanding   4 points
B = Above Average   3 points
C = Average   2 points
D = Needs Improvement   1 point
F = Severe Deficit   0

tect when the child is physically ill, having trouble at school, or for other reasons needing special attention. Communication with the child includes an appreciation of the child's perspective. Parents who excel in job skills probably have taken time to learn about child behavior, development, and enrichment needs. These parents can adapt effectively to the child's various developmental stages and changes such as family relocation or divorce.

Child Care:
Nurturance, protection, security; to feed, clothe, keep clean, provide shelter and comfort

Behavior Management:
Help child develop internal control, delay gratification, appropriate socialization; exercise control, discipline, reinforce positive behavior, model acceptable behavior, teach, train, and respond consistently to the child

Enrichment:
Provide a stimulating environment, cultural and social experiences, to stimulate learning, add interest and fun to the child's life

Communication:
Interact in a sensitive and understanding manner, appreciate the child's perspective, respect child's feelings

Knowledge and Expectations:
Understand how a child develops; realistic expectations of child, appreciation of child's needs, interests and abilities; accurately assess child's strengths and weaknesses

Goals:
Sense what one hopes to accomplish as a parent and assess one's parenting relative to these goals

Flexibility:
Adapt to changing needs and issues as the situation and developmental stage requires; be able and willing to change what is being done when it is not working

Role

Positive parenting behaviors automatically come into play if the role of parent is highly valued. The parents' emotional investment is associated with pride, meaningfulness, and joy. More time is spent with the child helping him to assimilate the world. High marks here indicate that the parent feels responsible to be a positive adult example.

Emotional Investment:
Sense of pride, importance, and meaningfulness associated with being a parent

Time Commitment:
Parenting assumes a reasonably high ranking in one's personal agenda and time is spent appropriately

Joy and Satisfaction:
Pleasure in being the most important person to the child; enjoyment in being part of the child's world; sharing skills, knowledge, and values

Role Model:
Presence in style and behavior that enhances the child's emulation adults

Emotional Accessibility:
Emotional openness and rapport

Identification:
Presents values and world view in a manner that enables
the child to assimilate

Temperament

Subtle emotional nuances are often the most important
part of the parent-child relationship. The critical issue
isn't so much what you are doing (job) or the investment
(role), but the quality of the experience (temperament). It
describes the emotional climate of the child as created by
the parent. The parent who is accepting, relaxed, and patient probably will elicit those traits more easily from the
child than a parent who is confrontational, stressed, and
impatient. The good parent in this category provides the
child with guidance while supporting the child's independence and feelings.

Although job skills and the parenting role can by no
means be discounted, these categories will not yield positive results without proper temperament. Consider teaching a child the basic visual-motor skill of catching a ball.
Imagine a parent who focuses on the skill development in
a cold and critical manner. Compare this image with one
of a parent teaching the same skill while focusing on the
child in the spirit of play, fun, and acceptance. Clearly,
the child is learning much more than catching the ball.
He is learning how he is viewed by the parent, how to
value himself, and how he will behave when he is in the
teaching role.

Emotional Climate:
A psychological atmosphere that is warm, accepting and
relaxed; ability to cope with child's failures and shortcom-

ings with fairness and even temper; shield child from frustrations experienced by the parent

Patience:
Accept child's pace in learning and in functioning

Sensitivity to Child's Needs:
Ability to accurately read the child, to differentiate one's personal needs from the child's needs and feelings.

Control Maintenance and Relinquishment:
Provide control as needed, to let go as needed, support independence and responsibility

Perspective:
Maintain balance, differentiate what is important from what is trivial and to act accordingly

Crisis Management:
Respond to behavioral, social, and medical emergencies in a competent and emotionally even manner

Control of Self:
Modulated in emotional display, restrained in behavioral reaction

Report Card Evaluation

The Parent Report Card shows the complexities of parenting. "Straight A" parenting is not necessary for positive results. The paradox is that children gain from parental imperfections. Growing up includes learning to cope with stress, unreasonableness, unfairness, and other common lapses in human nature. The parent who never lapses denies a child the opportunity to experience variations of humanness. Having a parent who returns home from work in an irritable mood and in need of some time to wind down teaches the child to be sensitive to the needs of others. Imperfections, if not carried to excess, expose the child to mild adversity and help him to learn to react in appropriate ways. This is analogous to exposing the child to low doses of infectious material to acquire immunity.

A parental grade of C is usually adequate, but anathema to achievement oriented, college trained, middle-class Americans. How good must you be to be good? Even a smattering of Ds are okay if not in key areas. Ds in child care or emotional climate, especially during the first five years of the child's life, usually indicates poor parenting. On the other hand, Ds in the areas of perspective or flexibility may not result in personality damage. While not extolling the D rating, it is a matter of degree, age of child, and particular area needing improvement that should be considered. A few Ds on the record do not automatically relegate someone to the status of poor parent.

A grade of F in any area indicates a serious parenting deficit, so poor that it impacts adversely upon the child. Good parenting ends at the point in which the child is affected adversely and in a lasting way by parental inadequacy.

The bottom line—good parenting is not so hard to accomplish. A good parent's report card has no Fs and no more than a few Ds in non-critical areas at ages when the child is not particularly vulnerable to parental flaws. A rating of better-than-good includes some As and Bs. No child was ever hurt by an unduly patient parent who provided a super-enriched environment and had a high emotional investment in the child. But perfection is not the goal of parenting, and being far less than perfect is usually good enough.

Martin's (Chapter 1) first child was born three years before he received his doctorate degree; Martin was thirty-six years old. Three and a half years later, his second son was born. Recall also that Martin was a graduate student without the social, psychological, or financial means for raising a child. Sixteen years have passed since the agonizing decision to have children.

Martin had, from the beginning, a strong ego commitment to parenthood. He would be rated highly in most job skills and role qualities. He maintained a busy professional life that kept him away from his family most evenings of the week and lowers his grade in this area. The parameters of temperament are most troublesome for him. He usually can maintain a positive, emotional climate, but he also can be impatient and insensitive to his children's needs. Martin has failed to protect his children from the stress and financial worry of the marriage. He can be brusque and highly critical in hurting ways. Martin is concerned that such incidents have eroded his sons' confidence in themselves. He is also concerned about providing his children with meaning in their lives.

None of Martin's parenting limitations merit an F, although one or two Ds in the temperamental area are appropriate. He is a good parent with a B-minus rating.

Peggy is a young mother whose only son, David, lives with his adoptive father in a distant state. She married when she was a pregnant teenager. The marriage failed when her son was still an infant. Her second husband adopted the boy, and the two developed a good relationship. Peggy divorced a second time, and the boy became defiant and unmanageable. He performed poorly in school and engaged in delinquent activities. Peggy was a student nurse trying to develop the means to support her family. But her academic needs conflicted with parenting needs. The stresses intensified when Peggy acquired a live-in boyfriend. While he was supportive and concerned, he was perceived as a rival by her son. Her son's rebellion probably was his way of discharging internal tensions and anger. Nevertheless, it became impossible for Peggy to parent, and David's escalating behavior problems developed into serious authority problems. Fortunately, the ex-husband assumed parental custody. Peggy maintained close contact with David including lengthy visits during the winter holidays and summer vacation.

Peggy is a good person and a loving parent. But her inability to construct a decent life with her son didn't stem entirely from parenting inadequacies. Her son was a strong-willed, demanding child who was threatened by Peggy's relationships with men. Had he been a mellower child, the problems may not have developed. Difficulties are created by a combination of the parent's situation, and the nature of the child in the context of the times and circumstances. Peggy had difficulty with behavior management, emotional investment, and time commitment. Joy and satisfaction were lacking in daily parental responsibilities, and she was somewhat insensitive to her child's needs. She was adequate in other areas, but not enough to compensate for the Ds. To her credit, she was aware of her limitations and took difficult, but appropriate, steps to rectify the situation. Peggy rates a C minus.

The value of the Parent Report Card lies in delineating and organizing various components of parenting. It defines these components and evaluates parenting performance. A parent who doesn't feel good about a rating can change, do it differently. Do it better. The Report Card focuses upon and mirrors back to the parent what is usually taken for granted, restores control to the parent, and presents choices that were lost when function became automatic and unthinking.

The Report Card limitation is that it gives insufficient insight into the concept of a good parent. We know that bad parenting can damage children physically and mentally. But in less extreme cases, it is exceedingly difficult to predict how the quality of parenting affects children. Parents can be good in some ways, bad in others. Good people can be thwarted by impossible situations. All manner of forces, influences, and stresses interplay beyond the parent's control, and even luck may be a factor.

Parents were invited to rate themselves on the Report Card to better chart their pluses and minuses. Hopefully, rating yourself on the Report Card was an awakening exercise. Situation and contextual variables should not be overlooked. This will help us to look kindly upon our weaknesses and to forgive our lapses. Children can survive most of our limitations. Knowing this, let's consider what parents contribute to the way children grow up.

Chapter 4

Why Grow Up?

Growth. . .requires courage, will, choice and strength in the individual as well as protection, permission and encouragement from the environment, especially for the child.
Abraham Maslow, *Toward a Psychology of Being*, 1962

As tough as it is to be a parent, it is equally tough to be a child. As hard as it is to live with them, it is just as hard for them to live with us. Every dilemma in the life of the parent mirrors a dilemma in the life of the child. If the job of parenting is the most difficult job of all, the job of growing up is not far behind.

Mother nature provides the impetus to develop and mature. The neonate enters the world with innate potential to grow and to strengthen. We develop capabilities for increasingly complex and sophisticated mental and physical activity. The equipment of life matures and we are impelled to try it out. Each advance provides opportunities for new tests and challenges.

The processes of growth may be viewed as steps along which we advance. Every aspect of human endeavor contains potential to develop. The child psychoanalyst, Anna Freud, writes of advancing along developmental lines. Motor development progresses from sitting to crawling, walking, and running. Its highest forms are expressed by ballet dancers and world class athletes. Language develops from goo-goo, ga-ga to the words of Shakespeare. The developmental line concept can be applied to each aspect of personality development. Ms. Freud refers to the advance from irresponsibility to responsibility, from dependency to emotional self-reliance, from egocentricity to companionship.

Despite the potential to grow, the process is not fully realized in many dimensions of growth. Most of us are neither poets nor accomplished athletes. Nor do we become all that we can be.

The psychologist, Abraham Maslow, maintained that every person has an essential nature of needs, capacities, and tendencies. We are impelled to actualize this nature, fulfill potentials, and develop into maturity. These ends have been accomplished by the self-actualized person. The vast majority progresses only part of the way.

What stops progress along a developmental line? In a sense we apply the Peter Principle* and advance to the level of our incompetence. As an issue is resolved or function mastered, we are freed to take the next step. But if we sense we cannot succeed at that level, there is no incentive to give up our security and risk failure at the next

---

*Dr. Lawrence J. Peter's, the Peter Principal, represents the idea that individuals in a hierarchical structure will continue to advance until they reach their level of incompetence.

level. An intermediate level skier will avoid the challenge of the advanced slope if experience or intuition tells her she may break her neck by trying. A young adult, secure in the comfort of his parents' home, may resist emancipation for fear of not having the skills to make it on his own.

Knowledge of growth progression can act as a stimulus to growth. Sensing that higher levels of maturity can be reached communicates that more work lies ahead. Without such knowledge, growth is blocked. But aging continues, and the discrepancy between social and chronological development becomes clearer with time.

We can all think of individuals who behave and experience events in a manner similar to those of a much younger age than themselves. Many have difficulty acting their age.

Amy is nine years old. She sits tightly bundled in her oversized jacket. Inside the right hand pocket is a tiny stuffed rabbit which accompanies her everywhere. It is comforting to touch and helps her through the ordinary stuff of her day.

———

Thirteen year old Matt bolts into the office, hyper and silly. He runs to the window, fiddling impulsively with such vigor that the blinds are ripped from the brackets.

———

A forty year old, professional business woman and the mother of three children, dreads the thought of visiting grandmother. The old woman is in the habit of baking sweet rolls for her guests and expects them to awaken at 6:00 am to "get 'em while they're hot." Grandma's feelings would be hurt and she would think you ungrateful, if you prefer sleeping in.

———

And then there is sixty-one year old Clem, at war with
his neighbors and any authority that he encounters. Clem
blames them all for obstructing his life and preventing
him from achieving the great things that he was meant to
accomplish.

While these particular examples are drawn from actual
clinical files, they represent behaviors and attributes that
are rather commonplace in everyday life. These are examples of people behaving as if significantly younger than
their chronological age. There is nothing unusual about a
three year old fondling a stuffed animal, playing with window blinds, being reluctant to displease grandmother,
squabbling with playmates or adults who are perceived to
be unfair. These actions are taken for granted and accepted as normal for a three year old. But they strike out
at you and are impossible to ignore when they are exhibited by older people. How often have we felt or said, ".My
God, so and so is behaving just like a baby."

We have standards and expectations for behavior at particular ages. What is acceptable at one age is entirely inappropriate later on. No one is concerned about a one year
old wetting herself. Continuing at age ten is reason for
concern. A toddler misbehaving in a restaurant may be an-
noying but accepted as normal. Similar behavior by an
older person would be viewed not only with annoyance
but also with alarm. A ten year old living at home, asking
permission and complying with parental wishes is far less
deviant than a forty year old in the same situation, behaving in the same way.

Examples of people who are arrested in personality development are abundant. Business people realize the differ-

ence between a person with twenty-three years of experience and a person with one year of experience twenty-
three times over. One learns and develops from
experience becoming capable of higher levels of contribu-
tion. In contrast, the other does not grow from experiences and thus, is incapable of reaching a higher level.
These common sense observations reflect what personality theory has to say about emotional growth.

One of the earliest and most profound emotional issues
of childhood is basic trust. This issue arises in the infant's
experience of early nurturing. If the nurturing parent is
perceived as warm, relaxed, and reliable, a mutually gratifying relationship is experienced. This primary encounter
during a time of total dependency results in an emotional
experience of benevolence and satisfaction. The inference
incorporated into the child's developing world view is a
giving, trustworthy reality. A fundamental attitude of
trust then emerges. With such an attitude established, the
infant likely assumes trustworthiness in other relationships and is ready to invest in succeeding developmental
issues and take the next steps in emotional development.

Consider the infant whose early nurturing experiences are
negative. The nurturing parent is tense, begrudging, and
unreliable. This experience is translated by the child into
feelings of uncertainty and insecurity. The child begins to
understand the world as a harsh and untrustworthy place.
The developmental issue has not been satisfactorily resolved. The infant develops into a person who is hostile
and on guard and expects to be let down. Emotional energy can never be fully invested in the succeeding developmental issues because the infant continues to seek
infantile gratification in all succeeding relationships. Dis-

trust becomes a fixed element in any relationship that is developed.

Growth Curves Illustrated

Growth curves illustrate the course of development for any dimension of personality. Figure 4.1 represents a composite of personality elements. Imagine the progress of two hypothetical children. Norma's curve illustrates normal growth. Dahlia is a person whose growth is delayed. Behavioral characteristics at various ages can be compared. This will illustrate how the life trends of these two children become more discrepant with advancing age. The theme of Norma's life is maturation of emotionality,

Figure 4.1 Normal and Arrested Developmental Lines

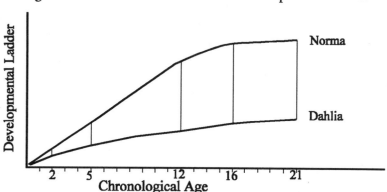

interests, and interpersonal expectations. For Dahlia, it is stagnation and entrapment.

Age Two
At age two, there may or may not be discernible differ-

ences between the two children. Researchers have found that from birth temperamental characteristics are apparent. These will contribute to and shape a child's response to the environment. Norma is gregarious, easy to satisfy, able to venture forth and explore. It is gratifying to be her parent.

We imagine Dahlia to be cranky, clingy, shy, and difficult to manage. She has difficulty developing a sleep pattern and is a fussy eater.

Age Five
The children are toilet trained by age five, but Dahlia has occasional lapses. Both children are entertained by television. Norma is excited to go to nursery school. She dresses herself and is eager to join the activities. Children like her, and she easily shares. Her projects are interesting and creative.

Dahlia resists getting up and she likes her mother to dress her. She has trouble separating and does not enjoy the school experience. She continues to be shy and she has little initiative. She is dependent on the teacher for ideas.

Age Twelve
Twelve year old Norma has developed many interests. She is motivated to do well in school and she takes pride in completing her projects. Much time is spent on the telephone and she does not like it when limits are set. She is not always agreeable, but she can argue in a reasonable way. She does not stay upset for long and she is forgiving. She earns money by babysitting and saves a portion of her money.

Dahlia spends much of her time watching television. She cannot wake herself in the morning and is unpleasant to those around her. She frequently complains of illnesses and seems to welcome opportunities to miss school. She procrastinates and argues about the silliest issues. She is teased and scapegoated by other children. She is generally in a bad mood.

Age Sixteen
Sixteen year old Norma has mastered several skills and is always busy. She has a driver's license and manages freedom in a responsible manner. Her friends are acceptable to her parents, and she has begun to date. Norma thinks about her future and is taking steps to enhance her prospects. Her relationships with adults tend to be positive.

Dahlia continues to watch much television. She is bored and moody. She is lacking in initiative but resents others who try to encourage her. She has few interests and does poorly in school. Like her friends, she skips classes and is considering dropping out. She uses drugs and alcohol. She is sexually active and casual about it. She does not like to think about her future. She is secretive and distrusting of adults.

Age Twenty-one
At twenty-one, Norma is about to graduate from college. She has a good sense of herself and what she wants from life. She is an interesting person who is appealing to others. Friendships are sustaining as are her romantic involvements.

Dahlia sleeps until awakened by her crying infant. She and her mother are raising the child. Tension and depression characterize the household. Dahlia does not have a driver's license nor a G.E.D. Devoid of interests, she fills her time watching television. Her few friends are unreliable and take advantage of her. She is often lonely. Her social life centers around parenting classes and drug rehabilitation meetings.

These composite life stories depict the difference between growth-striving and growth-resistant individuals. Many issues are raised in considering the developmental outcome.

To what extent is the outcome inevitable? Is it possible to change the course of events, and, if so, by what means? Our viewpoint is that people are instrumental in shaping events that contribute to how they turn out. Some have it easier than others. But even those who have personal shortcomings or live in tough circumstances have the capacity to realize their potential and lead wholesome lives. The process begins early in life.

There is nothing automatic about emotional development. The nature of experience shapes the manner in which not only reality but also the self is perceived. This is also true of cognitive development. One milestone in cognitive development assumes utmost importance— *recognition of the self as an evolving being.* It is truly extraordinary to contemplate an innocent toddler, who has only recently learned to walk and talk, transforming into a being able to grasp the concept that he or she will grow and some day become an adult.

What does this recognition entail? Such a concept of personal growth implies a sophisticated understanding of the self, as it is at the time and as it will be in the future. Projection of the self into the future involves concepts of time and of changes over time. To imagine oneself twice as large, in roles that are beyond present capacity is high level mental development. The emotional reactions associated with this conceptual understanding, must be considerable. This is not to say that a child is awe-struck as the future is contemplated. Perhaps the children of philosophers react in such a manner. In a less spectacular way, ideas of future growth probably excite, confuse, and generate apprehension. Given all that is implied conceptually and emotionally, we must consider that among the more remarkable statements of human assertion is the youngster saying, "When I grow up, I will be a mommy/daddy/doctor."

Children grasp not only the concept of personal growth but also its implications. Psychoanalytic theory asserts that as the self becomes sexually identified and projected into the future, the child imagines a relationship with the opposite sex parent and competition with the same sex parent. This obvious source of anxiety is believed to have a considerable influence on future development. The dilemma was handled rather deftly by my older son.

> At about three and one-half years of age, Seth returned from a birthday party with a hat that was shaped like a crown. He was the king and he announced that he'd marry Mommy, who would be his princess. "But if Mommy marries you," I protested, "what will become of me?" "Well," he suggested, "you can be the mailman."

> About the same age, my son was playing out a doctor fantasy. To participate in his fantasy, I came home one evening feigning illness. Flopping on his bed, I moaned "Doctor, doctor, I need a doctor." Seth, appearing quite anguished, confessed, "I used to be a doctor, but now I am a fireman." Clearly, he was no longer able to treat my illness and only my spontaneous recovery alleviated his apprehension.

These examples are commonplace. Children as young as two years of age act out adult roles. The first appearance of these fantasies marks the recognition of growth potential. These early attempts at adult role playing are innocent. They present a child's view of adult functioning that is charming to behold. The child is typically the hero of this personal fantasy. But as the concept of adulthood develops, the child soon begins to realize that it is not a simple matter to strive to be adult. As the encounter with my regal son demonstrated, there are pitfalls along the way. For not all daddies may be satisfied to be the mailman. Then what? Some dads might retaliate by withdrawing love or physically defending their place in the family. The Oedipal dilemma this scenario depicts may be the most dramatic and widely discussed of the factors in psychological growth, but it is not the only one.

Other factors influence the course of future growth. Much of fantasy play occurs within a social context. In simple games of house, children battle about who will assume what roles. There may not be room in the game for more than one hero. In one case, a younger brother was excluded from the play unless he was willing to be the baby. In another, a nine year old girl unwillingly became the maid. Another experience frustrated a seven year old girl. She spent hours preparing her materials for a game of school. Her friends simply declined to be her pupils. The battle that followed was an unhappy experience for all.

While these experiences may be considered merely unfortunate consequences of growing up, they are much more. For they represent what can happen to personal fantasy as it is projected into social reality. Some children are able to assert their personal fantasy within the peer culture with success. They become mommy or daddy, rather than the baby or the maid. Others can persuade their playmates to be the students, so they can be the teacher. For those who are successful, reality confirms the fantasy. They can be what they set out to be; the hero. But for the other children the fantasy is hindered. They are faced with a dilemma, for they are accepted only on condition that they give up their own fantasy for something less desired. They can belong, but they must give up the hero role. If experiences of this type begin to dominate, these children develop doubt in their capacity to grow up successfully. This does not mean they are consciously aware of their doubt, but they may dislike those who succeed in realizing the hero fantasy. Or, they avoid situations in which the issue may arise and routinely defer to the other children's wishes. Thus, an experience necessary for growth is lost. Some actually verbalize that they have no desire to grow up. They prefer to remain children. But even if they are unable to say so directly, their behavior clearly indicates the way they feel.

The medium of athletics provides another opportunity for projecting personal fantasy onto a social stage. Athletes, like policemen and firemen, are held in high esteem by children. They are clear symbols of adulthood. Their activity is on public display and what they do illustrates the motor development of early childhood. It is no wonder that athletes are held in such high esteem by children. The fantasy is intensified by outfitting children in replicas of adult uniforms and naming teams after those used in adult leagues. Most children are seduced by the athletic fantasy and see athletic prowess as highly desirable. The good athlete is admired and accepted by peers. The athletic fantasy is validated by success and the admiration of others.

The child who is a poor athlete is often despised, rejected, and subject to ridicule. While such a child has likely entered the competition in belief that he was potentially major league material, the fantasy is shattered by the experience. Many children with minor gross motor delays or other such impairments are subjected to cruel and humiliating reactions from their teammates. The effects of this can be traumatic and damaging. One eight year old boy was convinced that he was not only a terrible soccer player but a terrible person who deserved the unkind treatment he was given. He rejected his parents' attempts to support and comfort him. All they accomplished was to lose their credibility in his eyes. Their comments were nullified by the truth obtained in peer society.

Even more complicated experiences can be encountered in school. The classroom and school yard test fantasies in settings provided by adult authority and peer society. Being a good student may mean a validation of personal fantasy, compliance with parental expectations, or approval by teachers and respect from classmates. This is not always the case. In some cultures a good student is rejected by peers who may resent the student's success or ridicule any interest in learning.

It is not only the good student whose academic performance targets him. A poor student may face even more adverse reactions from peers and develop attitudes about the self that are difficult to change.

> A learning disabled nine year old was taunted by playmates who convinced him that he was retarded. His inexperienced therapist challenged this false belief directly.

"Mike," he said, "I am a psychologist. Psychologists are experts who know who is and who is not retarded. I am telling you, as an expert, that you are not retarded." Mike was not convinced, "Some expert you are," he rejoined.

A child's response to the birth of a sibling has important consequences for future psychological development. In the ideal scenario, a child is able to identify with parenting attitudes relating to the new baby. The child can forge a more expansive relationship with the parents if he or she feels a part of the parenting team. The neonate is viewed as an added attraction, a source of excitement, a curiosity, and a potential playmate. Privileges of being the older child are valued and the responsibilities appreciated. This ideal, like infinity, is only approachable, never fully realized. But where the ideal is approached within reason, the birth of a sibling can provide an impetus to grow. It is interesting that in some societies the expectations of such a response and outcome are built into the culture. In the barrios of the Philippine islands, for instance, it is commonplace for children to raise younger siblings. Four year olds care for three year olds, three year olds care for the two and younger set. Whatever other problems that such arrangements may beget, the reaction to sibling birth apparently stimulates personal psychological growth.

The opposite is seen in some families. The birth of a sibling impedes growth and in some cases reverses it. Sometime, the primary reaction is to see the neonate as a threat. This is not necessarily apparent. Many parents can recall initial excitement and joy on the part of the older sibling. But, that was before the child recognized the implication of the new baby. Then the hostility began to emerge; often in the guise of caring. Older sisters have been known to hug the baby until he turns blue; pinch him affectionately until the screams of pain reach a parent's ears, and playfully careen the stroller right into the wall with gleeful abandon. One four year old patient summarized the issue quite cogently. Upon finishing her therapy hour she confronted her two year old brother in the waiting room, balloon in his hand. She ripped it from his hand, pushed him to the floor, and climbed into his stroller. Her stunned father was at a loss to respond. Older brothers can be equally cruel to baby sisters. They tend, however, to be more direct in their aggression. No pretenses at all about caring. Many simply do not like girls, and they show their disdain with open aggression like a punch in the stomach.

As the brother of a sister four years my senior, I have difficulty remaining objective. But based on clinical and personal experience, the older child senses a loss of control as the implications of the new baby are realized. Parents no longer dote on the older child exclusively. He begins to feel ignored. Attention accorded the neonate is perceived as rejection of the older child. The hurt can be alleviated by hurting the younger child and control is re-established by physically dominating the new child. Some children believe the parents' attention can be regained by emulating the baby. This regressive behavior reveals what the older child actually experiences. It communicates the loss of exclusiveness, specialty, and love. This loss is subconsciously attributed to being the older child. To regain what has been lost, older children sometimes feel they must revert to infantile behaviors.

Rivalry between siblings often begins to take the form of who can out-baby whom. The size and strength advantage of the older child is offset by the parental protection received by the younger. But in the battle for top baby, growth is stifled. No one can see the advantages of growing up. Whoever grows up loses. Independence, mastery, and emancipation represent the losing hand. One succeeds by not succeeding, and psychological growth is interrupted.

The intensity of such sibling battles is aggravated when the younger child outshines the older.

> A learning disabled ten year old expressed feelings of humiliation and bitterness attributed to the fact that his younger sister was able to read better than he. Mack expressed his rage by finding excuses to physically attack her. But whatever satisfaction he obtained by his superiority in the fight could not compensate for the pain be experienced for being slow, even though he actually scored in the average range of intelligence. Similar feelings were generated from his peer interactions and interfered with these relationships. Despite Mack's intelligence, he was achieving poorly in school, and he was making little progress in learning therapy. He sensed that he could not successfully grow, and his behavioral and academic problems acted out what he sensed.

What is it that determines a child's response to the younger sibling? Three patterns for regressive responses are suggested from my clinical experience.

- ◆ The first arises from a situation in which a first born is highly valued and amply parented causing close, gratifying, and exclusive ties to be forged between parent and child. The birth of the sibling and its needs for parenting provides an overwhelming contrast between what was and what now is. The first born feels betrayed and threatened to such a high degree that he has difficulty accepting the reality of the multi-child family.

◆ The second stems from the vulnerable child's need for parenting; the one who is physically at risk or learning disabled or handicapped some other way. Such children are often realistically dependent on parents. They sense themselves to be damaged and feel replaced by a more competent or healthy and younger rival. There is a strong tendency to use this weakness to gain advantage in the sibling rivalry.

◆ Third are older children who hold onto family life as a refuge from frustration in the peer culture. In such cases, the younger child becomes the older child's substitute for peer involvement, but the interaction is frequently immature and fraught with hostility.

———

Events in the classroom and on the playground and experiences with siblings, peers, and adults accumulate. From them we learn about ourselves. Whether valid or not, this information influences our image of who we are. We may learn that we can go so far and no further. Such a conclusion can obstruct the impulse to grow. The risk of failure is too great to give up the security of what has been attained. If we conclude that we cannot fit in or be self-reliant, cannot aspire, create, or live a rewarding life, progress will be delayed along few or many developmental lines. We have now narrowed the possibilities and opted for safety. Such stifling of growth can constrict one's life. Most of us have progressed sufficiently along sufficient developmental lines to live reasonably good lives. That is not to say we have become all we can be.

So as we have seen, children develop a sense of their capacity to grow. This unconscious attitude shapes and filters experience and directs the speed and course of future growth. With a positive attitude, the child is able to challenge the self, take risks, and seek new experiences. On the other hand a negative attitude leads to withdrawal from challenges, risks, and new experiences. Such a child holds onto what has been achieved and remains psychologically stagnant.

Growth requires direction and confidence. In the absence of direction, growth is misguided. In the absence of confidence it is suspended. Internalization of these factors is crucial. The subtle nature of the process compels a parent's focus on possible intervention, and as parents can influence the process, it warrants detailed discussion.

Direction of growth is first apparent in the child's hero fantasies. The hero is an immature concept of adulthood. The hero reflects simple impressions of adult attributes such as strength, courage, and honesty. Influencing the development of these hero fantasies are cartoons and athletic events.

But more immediate and in the long run more decisive, parents are providing the input from which the child learns the nature of adult experience. Parents provide the details that articulate the subtleties of adulthood. The child develops an internal representation, a mental impression of adulthood which we call the Adult Ideal. This is what the child perceives as adult.

Adult Ideal: An Internal Guide to Personal Growth

The Adult Ideal is the conceptual centerpiece of growth. It is a child's impression of adulthood formed by the child's ideas of the standards, expectations, and style of an adult life. It functions as an internal guide to psychological growth by providing direction and incentive to grow. These qualities of the Adult Ideal impact psychological development.

A Triple-A Rating: Elements of the Adult Ideal

Attractiveness
What is so good about growing up? To the young child, an adult typically implies very attractive qualities. Most games that emulate adults are exciting, full of adventure, and just plain fun. Fantasies take the form of space adventurers, including female astronauts, as well as the old stand-bys of cowboys, cowgirls and soldiers. The adult role models are inevitably on the side of good. Only rarely does anyone agree to be the bad guy/gal. Bad is generally imaginary and impersonal.

Children are often fortunate to know adults whom they greatly admire. Perhaps it is a parent or other relative, friend, neighbor, scout leader, teacher, or coach. With some children the person of admiration is a cultural hero, not personally known. Joe Louis, Amelia Earhart, John Kennedy, Martin Luther King, Kathryn Hepburn, and Albert Einstein were heroes familiar to older generations. Today's children may settle for lesser heroes, not necessarily real: The Terminator, Indiana Jones, and Wonder Woman. Special adults or heroes inform children of the good to be anticipated by growing up. Such role models and heroes provide a powerful incentive to grow up.

The positive view of adulthood is challenged by experience. Children encounter many adults unworthy of admiration or adults reacting to circumstances in unattractive ways. Many of society's heroes turn out to be less than attractive. Parents can be unreasonable, irritable, and devoid of fun. Supportive and fun adults are also mean, unfair, and corrupted.

Adulthood implies obligations, responsibilities, unrewarding work, and eventually sickness and death. When seen in this light can anyone blame a child for not wanting to grow up?

Both positive and negative influences impact the Adult Ideal. The balance of influences determines whether the Adult Ideal is attractive or not. The one leads to growth striving; the other to growth resistance.

Attainability
Attainability is the second of the Triple-As. If the Adult Ideal is essentially negative; there will be little desire to strive for adulthood. Alienated youth, for example, reject values and standards that others consider to be mature. But identification with adulthood is not sufficient to insure wholesome striving. Some children may be intimidated or overwhelmed by the attractiveness associated with adulthood. A boy may greatly admire his father and wish he could become just like dad but deep down inside feels he lacks what it takes. Such a child may give up striving to grow up, no matter what his personal accomplishments are.

Thus, if adulthood standards are too high, a child is likely to sense that he is incapable of attaining them. Overrating parents or heroes has negative effects on growth.

> Alex, the slightly-built son of a prominent, ex-marine father maintained infantile attitudes and developed overtly feminine mannerisms. He took no responsibility for broadening his own life and rejected his parents' attempts to encourage him to do so.

——

Donald, a symphonic player in a second line orchestra, is a composer of serious classical music. Despite his accomplishments, the musician was not fulfilled because he did not live up to the ideal of the father, who had been a player with the New York Philharmonic under Toscanini.

These are good examples of people whose concepts of adulthood were so exaggerated that it was not possible to attain the ideal. Too much attractiveness in a parent or hero can lead to doubt about attainment. This stifled Alex in his growth. He chose to avoid striving to be manly, as represented by his father. The symphonic player, Donald, could not appreciate his own accomplishments. He did not measure up to an unrealistic ideal and was chronically depressed.

Articulation
The Adult Ideal must be well defined, comprehensive, and understandable. There is more to being an adult than symbols, mannerisms, and attitudes. Adulthood implies deepened appreciation of the human condition, broadened perspectives about life, compassion for the plight of others, and the molding of intelligence and experience into wisdom. This view of adulthood means more than wearing a firemen's hat, handling a cigarette in a particular manner, or speaking in an authoritarian voice. The Adult Ideal evolves, becomes more articulated, and offers new possibilities. This provides more subtle and nuanced guidance in striving toward adulthood.

Direct experience with mature adults is a primary source of the evolving Adult Ideal. A young child is not perceptive of the subtle characteristics of a mature adult. But, in the presence of the mature adult, he gains recognition and appreciation of the subtle aspects of adulthood and incorporates these into a personal concept of the adult. In contrast, a child of equal capability in an atmosphere devoid of mature, subtle adult influences has no opportunity to experience these qualities. Sadly this child is less likely to include these subtle qualities into the personal Adult Ideal.

Personal experience in surviving disappointment or adversity can also build character and lead to a better understanding of the Adult Ideal. Peer influences or abstract experiences such as reading may add positive aspects. But the primary source of articulating the Adult Ideal is the influence of mature adults.

The implications for parents are immediate. What kind of Triple-A rating do I present to my child? If I express attractive qualities my child will want to identify with them. If I do not, the child will reject what I stand for. The parent who is remote, intimidating, or unavailable communicates that the child is incapable of attaining what attracts him. It is best to be there for your child, have fun, and let him win once in a while. This shows that he can be what he admires. Be a complete person, for better or worse. Your display of emotion, interest, and activity helps him to articulate a fuller dimension of adulthood. You are allowing your child the opportunity to develop a mature Adult Ideal and to broaden his perspectives and possibilities.

The Adult Ideal provides impetus and direction for growth. The hero fantasy expresses the child's aspirations and concepts about adulthood. Experiences with the hero fantasy determine the prospects for realizing the fantasy. Most of us learn that we will not become the hero. Modifications are then in order. This can occur without stifling the growth impulse. Many wholesome solutions are possible. But in unfavorable circumstances, growth can be blocked.

Once we sense that we have progressed as far as possible, we have, in effect, renounced the hero fantasy. In its immature form, the hero depicts an adult who performs daring deeds, is the star of the game, a savior of one or another kind. I have used the hero concept as a metaphor to describe the process of becoming the most that we can be along many developmental lines. In terms of responsibility, self-sufficiency, and independence, the hero is the one who has met the challenges along the way. In this sense, we are no longer discussing astronauts, football stars and champions. We are talking about learning disabled children who master their frustrations in the classroom and compensate for their inabilities. We are talking about children of divorce, latchkey kids who rise to the occasion and pitch in to contribute to the family. We are talking about youngsters growing up on the mean streets, yet avoiding the pressures and temptations that can lead them astray. For those whose responses are less than heroic, there are other wholesome solutions that lead to meaningful lives.

Wholesome Accommodations to Reality

The Hero Solution

The hero is the child who is able to project the personal fantasy into the social stage with success. Messages learned in the street are consistent with the positive messages learned in the family. The child senses the self in the number one position and this position is accepted by others. The choice roles in group fantasy and games accrue to the hero. Accommodation to reality is easy because reality is pleasant. It is the dream come true. Nature, experience, and luck are kind to these children and the groundwork is set for them to lead productive and fulfilling lives. However, the outcome is not necessarily positive. Life frequently throws the hero a curve ball. So the reader need not be obliged to envy the hero.

The hero accepts his challenge which brings out his best. The learning disabled student commits time and effort to learn, despite his difficulty. The latchkey child pitches in, contributing to the well-being of the family. When old enough, he will get a job to pay his own way. The chronically ill child takes responsibility for maximizing good health and living as full a life as his condition allows. In each case, the challenge of adversity is confronted wholesomely.

The Sidekick Solution

Heroes operating in a vacuum are a lonely bunch. Hollywood has recognized this basic truism by providing John Wayne with Gabby Hayes. Batman had Robin. There is hardly a hero without a sidekick.

Sidekicks do not have it so bad. True, they hardly ever get the girl, and they are accorded less recognition and respect than the hero. But they do share the excitement of the hero's life and they are close to the action. Personal esteem and reflected glory come from close association with the hero.

Since the vast majority of people lack the qualities and experience of heroes, reality can be accommodated by modifying the basic hero fantasy and accepting the self in a lesser role. By this means, the child continues to engage reality and to remain involved in a gratifying way. The accommodation enables the acceptance of self without rancor or illusion. The process is accommodating the reality that one will not be the football star, the swashbuckling pirate, or the victorious conqueror of evil. It is bringing reality into line. The strength, size, speed, courage, and motivation are not there. Not many children fantasize themselves as an obscure technician at a remote Army base counting the days until retirement. The fantasy is of glory and heroism, serving good and destroying evil. There has to be a dramatic modification of the fantasy of the self as hero to enable the child to be fulfilled in the mundane circumstances of which most of our lives are composed.

As typically understood, a sidekick supports and assists a hero. In the sense that we use the term, the relationship is mutual. To children of adversity, the sidekick solution implies alignment with others for mutual benefit. The relationship of Helen Keller and Annie Sullivan illustrates the hero-sidekick joint venture. Ms. Keller, deprived of sight and sound, could not on her own transcend her limitations. Ms. Sullivan engaged in an heroic effort to teach Ms. Keller to compensate. Together they transcended the adversity.

All kinds of issues are wholesomely addressed by the sidekick solution. A shy child can be brought out of the shell by a sympathetic, assertive friend. Chronically ill children can find a role in the activities of healthier friends. Mentors, tutors, and big brothers can assist learning disabled, lonely, or undersocialized children. The partnership works for each.

Big Fish in the Little Pond

There are ways of stepping down to a level at which the hero fantasy can be maintained. It may not be Broadway but there is opportunity to be the star in community theater. Several frustrated actors of my acquaintance have become speech therapists and teachers of retarded children. Through these means they continue to perform, and to perform well, before captured and appreciative audiences. Many a Vince Lombardi fantasy is played out in Little League sports. Who said these programs were really for the kids? How many Boy Scout leaders behave like General George Patton? Fantasies can be preserved by providing lesser stages for their expression.

Geographic step-downs also enable people to pursue their star without giving up the basic fantasy. There are big leagues and minor leagues in every area of endeavor. If one is willing to shop for location, one has prospects for finding an opportunity to maintain the fantasy. Many people have shuffled off to Buffalo and settled in Peoria. It may not be too far off base to suggest that some of the vast transmigrations that characterize American history are fueled by the search for a location in which the basic hero fantasy can be preserved.

The solution as applied to children of adversity is a way of maintaining the status of a hero, but on a smaller scale. No matter how adverse a condition may be, one can find meaning and reward by helping others. Schools have found, for example, that problem students gain by helping others who are younger or in the same boat. Children of divorce or chronically ill children share their experiences and gain in the knowledge that they are helping others. An important and meaningful experience in life is to become a hero in the life of another. We all have the capacity to do so.

The Narrow and Select Solution

There may be little opportunity to maintain the hero fantasy, but there are ways of developing situations where one can be what one cannot be in most other situations. "A man's home is his castle" conveys this idea. If he needs to be the king, this may be the only opportunity to pursue the dream. Serious hobbyists, such as model railroaders, develop a narrow interest into an opportunity to play out their fantasies. If the stage cannot be found, then it can be built. A segment of reality can be carved out to provide the necessary gratification. "I may be nothing on the job, but when I get home, I am the King" or "Monday through Friday, I am nothing, but on Saturday night I swing on the dance floor."

The playwright, Moss Hart, in his autobiography *Act One* relates a meaningful experience that helped him appreciate himself and find direction in life. A sensitive and unathletic child, he was bullied, ridiculed, and excluded by his tough, aggressive peers. But one particular rainy day, the children in the neighborhood were bored and restless. Deprived by the weather of the opportunity for physical activity they lacked the imagination to entertain themselves. Moss rose to the occasion. He invented a story that fascinated the guys for hours. The next day, sunny and bright, the kids again recruited Moss to tell another story. Moss had found his niche. No longer a despised outsider, he was valued and included for what he had to offer.

Many underappreciated children can develop select areas of life that provide satisfaction for the self and interest to others. This is particularly true for children of adversity, many of whom squander hours engaged in activity that provides little long-term benefit. If instead of television and Nintendo, they could engage in self-improvement activities they may find enriching rewards down the road.

Long Range Pursuer

Some continue to pursue their personal fantasy despite repeated frustrations and disappointments. In a sense, they do not accommodate to a reality that indicates they cannot realize their personal dream. The basic hero fantasy remains intact and their life is given meaning as the pursuer of the dream. In the long run, it matters less that they succeed or fail than it does that they have persevered. They have settled for nothing less than being the hero of their fantasy.

This type of solution is wholesome in that the individual maintains belief in the self despite repeated messages from others that the dream is not realistic. The obvious courage and determination that is required to maintain the belief is admirable. However, there is some danger that messages from others are indeed valid and should these be ignored, the long range pursuer risks slipping into a life of illusion which may become psychologically unwholesome.

For the child of adversity to fit the bill of the long range pursuer he must have some sense of what he is pursuing. This implies that he has developed goals and will not be deterred by his adversity, frustration, or by discouragement. The pursuit of long range goals adds passion and meaningfulness to life. This is a wholesome solution for children of adversity. For some, it means overlooking the conditions of a particular adversity, to dream beyond the conventional. Others may focus on the problem of coping with the adversity. But in either case, the long range pursuer does not accept defeat.

All of these solutions can be wholesome to the extent that they enable one to express fantasies in gratifying and acceptable ways. The star is able to translate fantasy onto the best possible stage. He is a psychological big leaguer. The sidekick gives up the star or hero fantasy but gains satisfaction by assisting and reflecting the glory of the star. The sidekick stays in the big leagues in a supporting role. The big fish maintains the star fantasy but settles for a minor league assignment. Such a person is able to derive satisfaction by being the primary focus of a lesser light. The narrow selector finds compensatory areas for expressing hero needs. The long range pursuer perseveres.

Looked at in another way, the star is psychologically the head of the giant corporation. The sidekick serves as the loyal assistant manager. The big fish becomes the head of a little store, perhaps in an out of the way location. The narrow selector becomes a dragon master. The long range pursuer perseveres psychologically. These solutions are of course metaphorical. They express what happens psychologically as children's fantasies are projected onto a social stage and adjustments to reality become inevitable. The adjustments are internal, coming to terms with what one is able to become. Internal harmony results from the resolution of the discrepancies between fantasy and reality. Not all internal adjustments result in harmony, however, and those that are not are considered to be unwholesome.

Unwholesome Accommodations to Reality

Illusions

A fantasy may be preserved by avoiding tests of reality. Remember my kingly older son. He grew up to be awkward and unathletic. Inevitably, he lost interest in and dropped out of any endeavor that involved athletics. As a child, he shied away from bats, balls, racquets, and skates. At age ten, he announced his intention to compete in the Olympics. In delight, I suggested that he still had time to prepare himself for the events of his choice. Perhaps he could organize a practice and training program for himself. These suggestions, of course, dampened the aspiration. My realistic suggestions were threatening to the illusions that could only be maintained by never testing them. My son did become adept at swimming, bike riding, and video game playing. These provided outlets for the testing of fantasy in areas in which there was a prospect for success and failure would not be so public.

Rationalization is another mechanism that can preserve illusions. The person admits that he is not the hero, but it is a begrudging admission because of the failure to take full responsibility for this. One says, in effect, that "I know if it were not for circumstances A or B, I most certainly would have become the hero." The fault is in the stars and not in the self. As such, the fantasy is preserved, but the self is never fully accepted, for one can never completely fool the self.

Redefining Reality

There are children who avoid facing their limitations by rewriting what a particular experience is intended to be.

Some poor students convert the school experience from learning and socialization to defiance of authority and education. Instead of coming to terms with their difficulties in learning, these children translate the situation into something other than the truth. "It's not that I am a poor learner, but that I am a good disparager. School is my opportunity to display my disparaging talents and that is what I will do."

Poor athletes are often seen roaming the outfield, mentally elsewhere, or clowning at bat. It is as if they communicate, "I am a lousy ball player but a great comedian. The ball field provides a stage for my stand-up comedy act." These kinds of adjustments result in conflict with reality. As long as the conflict is perpetuated, the child can avoid dealing with the real issues and frustrations.

Despair

Some children conclude that they are no good. They are unable to accommodate reality in a wholesome manner and they have not invented protective self-deceptions. Such children are highly vulnerable. They allow themselves to be victimized. There is little gratification in their lives. There is no star to follow and no role in anyone else's fantasy. Neither have they developed sustained illusions to protect them from their despair.

The Choice

The strongest principle of growth lies in human choice.
George Eliot, *Daniel Deronda*, 1876

There are many factors that likely contribute to growth and various combinations these are undoubtedly involved in individual cases. The reason people grow up is that they choose to grow up. Those who chose not to grow up remain committed to immature perspectives which become increasingly inconsistent with their chronological age. Aging, after all, is a continuous process unaffected by whatever blockages occur in personality development, but personality grows only to the extent enabled by choice.

The idea that people, young children in particular, determine the extent to which they will psychologically grow may appear far-fetched. It is more puzzling to consider that the process involves choice or decision making. It is simply against the grain of the way we perceive young children to think them capable of making important decisions that will impact their entire lives.

Yet, before a child is old enough to say "no" he is old enough to make choices. Chief among these is the choice to grow or not to grow in a manner that the child determines. All children say "no," and its utterance is not sufficient criterion for differentiating the growth-striving from the growth-resistant child. But all children do not say "no" to the same degree nor with the same intensity. They do not say "no" to the same issues or outgrow the phase at the same time. Some children say "no" to separation, going to bed, and giving up the bottle. But not all do. Some children say "no" to limits, to stifled explorations, to exclusion from social events. Some children say "no" to everything. These various forms of nay-saying fall on both sides of the line. Some are saying "no" to giving up infantilism, others are saying "no" to the restriction of growth striving. Clearly, these are choices made by the child.

Older children may recognize that their behavior is viewed as babyish and they may personally agree with this assessment without the slightest concern or distress. Chil-

dren who remain invested in blankets or stuffed animals
are good examples. It is the thought of giving up this security object, not the thought that it is babyish to hold onto
it, that causes the distress. There are other children who
cannot give up watching television cartoons, even though
they have seen dozens of reruns of a particular cartoon.
They can recite the entire scenario from memory.

> A twenty-two year old hellion, the scourge of several
> Denver low-life joints and in constant trouble with the
> police, spends each Saturday morning, starting at 6:00
> a.m., regardless of hangover, watching cartoons on televi-
> sion.

Whether or not the choice to engage in such activity is
made on a conscious or unconscious level, it derives from
personal decision making. We realize this because we
know that as people grow chronologically and physically,
opportunities to expand horizons become more available.
It becomes possible to develop particular skills, to pursue
social relationships, and to engage in hobbies. There are a
limited number of hours in the day. Time spent in one
way precludes spending it in another. Thus, choice is involved in the selection of activity. We infer that these
kinds of choices reflect inner and likely unconscious attitudes toward growth itself. Choosing to watch television,
like those who were described above, is to hold onto the
safe and familiar at the expense of engaging in some new
or more challenging endeavors.

Attitudes about growing up are reflected not only in activity but also by the style in which the activity is pursued.
Many people use an activity as an avenue for expressing
highly infantile behavior. A seven year old therapy patient
enjoyed playing the "baby game." Through this game, he

affected the mannerisms and experiences of babyhood.
He lay on his back thrashing arms and legs, demanding to
be bottle fed and enjoying every moment of it. It was not
only the game he chose to play, but also the style of his
play that was disturbing. For other children who maintain infantile needs may reflect this without necessarily re-
gressing to the level of behaving so totally like a baby as
this boy did. Other children may assume infantile vocal
mannerisms or immature silliness in the course of pursuing an activity. They may cling to an adult, suck on a fin-
ger or perhaps wet themselves. Clearly, these are
mannerisms that reflect immature and growth-resistant
traits.

Children have the choice to do it differently. This is more
obvious in adolescents who go to the opposite extreme by
posturing exaggerated mannerisms that they perceive to
be adult. The girl who droops under the weight of the
make-up on her face and the macho guy walking with a
swagger and drawing casually on a cigarette are illustra-
tive. These adolescents choose to affect being older. Other
children may choose to act younger. What you pretend to
be is what you are, or strive to become. Choice is evident
in either case.

Parents are affected by choices made by their children.
Their reactions impact upon the course of future develop-
ments. Much is at stake beyond the specific matter at
hand. For the parent-child interaction shapes the child's
attitude toward growth, capacity to make good choices,
and confidence in judgment.

Recognizing that choice is an element of behavior at each
stage of development enables parents to promote growth.
The younger the child, the more difficult it will be to rec-

ognize the choice element and to respond wholesomely. Issues related to feeding, toileting, and sleep are most basic. How do we understand the child who is reluctant to eat or resists sleep? How do we respond? When dealing with such issues parental issues are heightened. For the parent, the issue is sustenance or health. But what is the issue for the child? He cannot tell us. The guesses that we make may be off the mark. Is there reason for alarm? Parents try to influence and even override children's choices. Obviously, they have their own ideas about the reasons the child is reluctant to do what they think is in the child's best interest. "Mother (Father) knows best" is a familiar expression through generations of American citizens. This may indeed be true in many cases. Yet there comes a time to yield, when a shift is necessary, when the child has to decide, even if mother does know best.

> Fourteen year old Barry bitterly complained that his mother insisted that he wear short pants instead of the jeans he had chosen to wear for hiking in the Arizona desert. Mother knew that Larry would overheat and ruin the excursion with his whining and complaining. She had the power to override his choice and no one could say that she was wrong. On the other hand, Larry was humiliated, cast into the role of a naive child, and resentful of his mother's control. This type of interaction was the rule, rather than the exception—one of an unending series that had alienated mother and son.

> ─────

> Lyle sought marital counseling within weeks of marriage. His mother continued to make decisions on his behalf and disregarded his wishes. Lyle had never learned to establish his independence, limit his mother's excesses, and trust his own decision-making ability. His new wife had a

clearer perspective of the damaging interference of her mother-in-law's relationship to her husband.

These rather extreme cases illustrate the common issue. A child grows successfully when he chooses to grow. As an infant he is already making choices subject to a parent's interpretation and influence. If she can correctly interpret his messages, she can respond to her child's needs and support his choices. But it is not always possible to do so. Then her response is not supportive of the choice. She coaxes food intake when he has gas or is not hungry. As he grows she may deny him the opportunity to make choices or to veto them. Thus while in charge of the most profound choice of all—to grow or not to grow—the child is deprived of decision-making opportunity. The issue of choice becomes an area of conflict. One grows, lacking confidence in his own choices, becomes passive and unable to make choices, feels deviant or guilty, loses sight of the differences between good and bad choices. Unwittingly she is choosing to teach him to fear growth.

It is probably true that a parent knows better. But that is not the only consideration. What carries more weight is the necessity for a child to gain experience in the decision-making process. At every stage of development, there are opportunities for children to make decisions. Recognizing and supporting these opportunities are crucial elements in parenting. Keep in mind that the quality of decisions made by an adolescent is determined by what happens much earlier in life. Look at it this way. How can you expect an adolescent to make good decisions about drinking and driving if throughout his life his opportunities have been limited, demeaned, or vetoed?

Temperament, environment, parents, and luck influence the choices made. They contribute but do not determine what the choice will be. For many children are able to grow, despite handicaps and adversity in their lives. There are obviously other forces at work guiding and giving impetus to growth. The key element is the unconscious attitude toward psychological growth. Its importance is in the influence it exerts upon the choices that impel or resist further growth. There are advantages in looking at growth from this perspective.

First, this unconscious attitude enables one to view problems in growing, not as technical maladjustments nor as the result of esoteric workings of the mind, but as part of the drama of life. "To grow or not to grow" states the issue. This simple statement is an inadequate summary of the complicated possible variations on the theme. Growing up is neither easy nor simple. But how an event is viewed and understood has some influence in shaping reactions and responses. The choice perspective enables parents to respond in a way that can facilitate the process of growth. For growth confronts the child with himself—the part that strives to grow against the part that resists. This view acknowledges that the responsibility for growth is the child's. If it is understood in this way, the relationship between parent and child can be structured to avoid the pitfalls encountered in many kinds of parent-child interactions.

The perspective of choice is optimistic because it implies flexibility, the possibility of undoing poor choices. In terms of issues as basic as growing up, it is possible to change one's mind. Thus, while it is true that we encounter our share of eighty year olds acting like three year olds and others who have failed to grow up along the way, we encounter too, those who have recognized the problem and are willing to change. Of course, the decision initially made to resist growth stems from experiences that generated anxiety, humiliation, failure and so on. The process of undoing the decision inevitably entails a confrontation with the past and a revisit with the pain. No one has said that growing up is easy.

Another advantage of a choice perspective is that with a knowledge of the factors that influence the choice, an emphasis is given, not to events per se, but to the interpretation that is given to events. Loss of a parent, chronic illness, exclusion by peers, unwholesome parenting, affect children in different ways. For some, the impact may be detrimental. For others it may be painful, but ultimately strengthening.

Chapter 5

The Path to Growing Up

Child rearing. . .is not just a matter of taking care of the baby and young child. . but of supporting the child's efforts to take care of himself.
Lois B. Murphy and Alice E. Moriarty,
Vulnerability, Coping, and Growth, 1976

"When I grow up. . . ." is a profound statement of human assertion. The child begins to experiment, playing out fantasies about adulthood. Experiences with real and fantasy adults shape a mental impression—the Adult Ideal. Continued experiences broaden and articulate the concept, providing direction and impetus to grow. The hero fantasy is projected onto the social stage in the form of games, sports, and schooling. Experiences inform the child about the prospects for success. An unconscious attitude forms. Expectations of future success enhance growth; expectations of failure impede it. These factors influence the decision to seek growth or not. Those striving to grow welcome opportunities to participate in maturing activities. Resistance to growth shuts off growth opportunities and leads to stagnation. The discrepancy among one's interests, behavior, emotional development, and one's chronological age widens. This can lead to the development of an emotionally arrested personality or clinical symtomatology.

The path to growing up is represented by Figure 5.1. It is a tool to help parents recognize growth problems. Implications and solutions to these problems are more easily dealt with when the problem area is identified.

Incentives to Grow Up

The Growth Model is a blueprint for psychological growth. The flowchart represents normal growth on the right and arrested, abnormal growth on the left. The centerpiece, into which all elements flow, is the Decision. People grow, to the extent that they choose and the chart details what influences their choices. Notice—the Decision is situated between Growth Striving and Growth Resistance. The choice is to grow when positive influences on the right outweigh negative influences on the left. Like a balance scale, the tilt is in the direction carrying the most weight. The two factors that directly impact the Decision are the Adult Ideal and Reality. These determine direction and confidence—the road map and fuel for growth. The specifics included in the Growth Model have already been discussed. A brief summary can help a parent better understand how these concepts can help troubleshoot growth problems.

Growth Recognition and Working Hypothesis

The analysis begins when a child first understands that he will grow and become somewhat other than he is. It is an amazing intellectual and emotional milestone. With understanding comes interest in experimentation. Child's play acts out concepts of future being. Various roles are assumed. It is great fun. The major influence on growth rec-

Figure 5.1   Psychological Growth Model

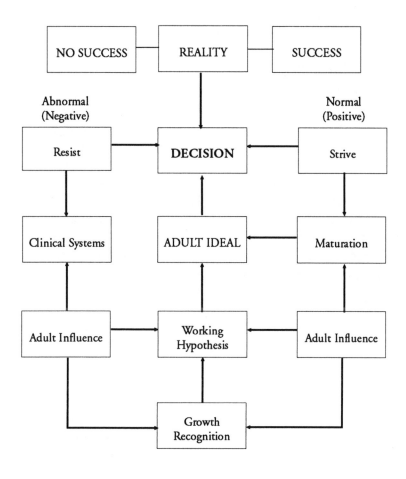

ognition is the direct experience the child has with important adults, most often parents, but also others who share
in his care. Both positive and negative experiences influence the nature of recognition. Hopefully, at the early
and ensuing stages, the good outweighs the bad.

Adult Ideal

Play and experience with adults provides a child with
ideas about adulthood. We know about the three As of
growth. If attractive and attainable, the child will emulate
positive attributes and his concept will mature and articulate. This is illustrated by the feedback loop on the right
side of the chart. It represents an ongoing process of generally positive experiences with adults and incentive to
strive to grow by seeking growth experience leading to further maturation. Compare this to the left side of the
chart. Weighted more toward negative experience with
adults, the child develops a concept of adulthood that
tips the scale toward Growth Resistance. The child acts
out his negative concept of the adult or develops aver-
sions to growth experiences. His decisions stifle growth.
Rather than maturation, they lead to clinical systems;
emotional arrest, depression, asocial behavior.

Reality

Also influencing the Decision are experiences in the real
world; the playground, schoolroom, athletic field. These
experiences create expectations of Success or No Success.
It is a confidence factor. The child lacking in confidence
avoids growth experiences and sets himself up to fail. The
opposite is true of the confident child. He welcomes new
challenges, takes risks, and enjoys the opportunity.

The Decision

Growth is the cumulative impact of choices made by children and supported by parents. Matters great and small provide growth opportunities. The flowchart acknowledges the importance of experience and of adult influence. It emphasizes the relationship among parenthood values, Adult Ideal, and growth decisions. The Decision is the point that integrates all these factors. Parenting, temperament, time and ego commitments are the primary Adult Influences. Recall the discussions of parenting and parenthood. It is now apparent that a parent's experience, dilemmas, conflicts, competing needs, ambivalences, and joys, not only directly impact the on-going relationship with the child, but were being digested, stored in memory, and shaping the Adult Ideal. In the child's mind the quality of the Adult Ideal contributes to the direction of growth. The feedback loop on the right depicts a continuous process of growth striving that leads to progressive maturation of the Adult Ideal. Negative adult influence (left side of the flowchart) impedes the process.

Once again it is important to emphasize that Reality impacts growth decisions. No matter how loving, supportive, and growth enhancing a parent's influence may be, experience in the real world, if negative, can erode confidence and stifle the growth impulse. The experience of the successful child is consistent with and validates the positive messages of supportive adults. These are ideal conditions for promoting growth. But negative experience outweighs supportive parent messages. In fear of rejection or failure, a child may prefer the safety and comfort of a supportive home environment. Good can be extracted from such difficulties if parental values, such as perseverance and courage, are expressed and incorporated into the Adult Ideal. This will be discussed further in the section on Adversity.

As a child grows older, the opportunity for independent action increases. By adolescence the capability for behavior impacting in profound ways has been attained. Choices to be made in adolescence have been determined by the cumulative effect of experiences from birth. Experience is destiny.

Emphasizing growth, the model directs parents to attend to new issues or to look at old issues in a new way. Socializing children and helping them to grow are the aims of parenting. With these aims in mind, the daily encounters with your child can direct responses to the growth issue. Some common parenting issues are now considered from the growth perspectives.

What's so good about growing up? Why would anyone even consider it? Children who resist growth are answering these questions in the negative. They see no gain in traversing the developmental lines and do not feel good about growing up. They resent, not welcome, the opportunity to grow. The process is experienced as onerous, not liberating. The child who resists growth is difficult to manage. He is content to stagnate—to put the responsibility for growth on the back of someone else, usually Mom.

The Growth Model assumes that no matter how strong the growth resistance, a kernel of growth striving is yet alive. It may be a flicker against the inferno of growth resistance. Two basic strategies are possible: (1) to extinguish the inferno, or (2) to nurture the flicker. The Growth Model suggests that the second approach is likely to be the more effective.

For how does one go about extinguishing an inferno? The usual tactics are threats and punishment. The parent is cast into the role of taskmaster and enforcer. A negative environment is established and in the process a child is prone to reject his parent. This impacts on the Adult Ideal. For the child is unlikely to perceive the parent as attractive and will reject parental values. How many slobs are the products of chore-oriented home environments?

On the other hand, support of growth striving casts the parent in the role of ally modeling the benefits of grown-up behavior. In this way a positive image is maintained which fosters identification and articulation of the Adult Ideal. No matter how resistant to growth the child may be, maintaining an alliance and exhibiting attractive qualities will enhance growth. A child wants to feel grown-up.

Eight year old Cynthia is a passive, growth-resistant child. She is unresponsive in psychotherapy, crawls into the fetal position and pulls her coat over her head. Her response to therapy mirrors her general attitude about life. The therapist acknowledges her discontent.

He points out that it is a problem for her to do what she does not like to do. He questions how she is dealing with her problem, suggesting that her response is like a little girl. By defining her actions as infantile (without using such a loaded term), he is attempting to alienate her from her behavior and to create discomfort. He then proposes a better way. The big girl sits up, looks at the therapist, tells him what she really thinks. She can tell him her reasons for not liking to come in. The prospect appeals to Cynthia. Soon she is sitting, smiling, and telling the therapist off. She is expressing herself, taking effective action, and acting appropriately. It feels good to act her age.

This is not a fool-proof tactic, but it has power to persuade many children to rise to the occasion. Should they
regress at a later point, they are reminded of their capacity to act their age. Notice that the child is not repri-
manded for not cooperating or being moody. She is
encouraged to express herself in an age appropriate manner. This is a positive interaction. It is kept positive even
if she is unresponsive. If not today, perhaps the next time
she will choose to act her age. Growth striving is supported, no matter what.

Responsibility for Growth

Children who resist growth, avoid experiences that facilitate it. Many are passive. They describe themselves as lazy
or forgetful. They show little interest in challenges and
new experiences. They languish in front of the television
set or play computer games. They have trouble rising in
the morning, getting ready for school, doing homework
and chores. Frantic parents are impelled to get the kid up,
prod him to get ready, see that the homework is done.
Schools are good at assigning a student's responsibilities
to the parent. A program developed by the teacher and
monitored by the parent is devised. But a clever, growth-
resistant child has no difficulty thwarting the program.
He forgets the assignment sheet or the book. He denies
that there is a project to work on.

The Growth Model emphasizes that the child has responsibility for his own growth. He makes the choices. He deserves full credit for successes and he owns up to poor
choices. There are natural consequences for his actions. In
working with families and schools, I emphasize that we
are a team. But the child is the captain of his team. If the
captain is out to lunch, it matters not what the crew is do-

ing. A child enjoys being the captain. It confirms his responsibility and it alleviates the guilt parents feel when they relinquish control.

Growth Problems vs. Authority Problems

The Growth Model assumes that resistance to taking developmental steps underlies the problems that develop. It is anxiety and a lack of confidence that stifle growth. Or, uncertainty and lack of direction lead children astray. Resistance takes the form of passivity, irresponsibility, and defiance. A concerned parent is frequently frustrated in her attempts to motivate, encourage, or coerce her child into action on behalf of himself. She is cast into the role of monitor, enforcer, and dispenser of punishment. Wittingly or not, the responsibility for his growth has become hers.

The basic growth problem has been transformed into an authority problem. The more she threatens, the more he resists. A downward spiral of negativity; threat, punishment, and increasing irresponsibility creates tension and ill will. It is easy for him to block her attempts to move him into action. His weapon is passivity. The more he does nothing, the more irritated and anxious she becomes. The spiral accelerates downward.

No one benefits. The child has finessed his underlying anxiety by converting his growth problem into an authority conflict. But he has lost sight of the fact that by winning the battle, he is losing the war. He is failing to take necessary developmental steps to prepare himself for a decent future. He is closing doors that may be difficult to open should he ever free himself from the trap. A parent engages the battle for various reasons. She is concerned.

Unless she rescues her child from himself, he will fail or get into serious trouble. It is difficult to renounce the rescue fantasy, despite experience of futility. The more she rescues, the more irresponsible he is. Mom may also react against her sense of his manipulations. No one enjoys being manipulated, especially by a child. It evokes anger and emotions are intensified. He threatens her authority, impelling her to defend her power and dignity.

The Growth Model reminds parents that the conflict is within the child, not between the child and parents. To accept the premise of an authority problem is to walk into a trap. The battles and conflicts are smoke, serving to obscure the real issues. The real consequences of a child's irresponsibility are not parents' punishments, but life's impact; school failure, entanglements with the authorities, lost opportunities. But even though these consequences may not be avoided, a child benefits if he accepts responsibility for the failure. That will not happen if the parent has been trapped into a power struggle and is viewed as the problem.

A parent is not advised to be uninvolved or indifferent. On the contrary, growth parenting is engaging. To avoid power struggles, one is creative in response. It requires patience, shrewdness, and the command of one's emotions. Issues are framed to promote, rather than to stifle growth. To accept the premise of an authority issue is to walk into a trap. It is not necessary to accept that premise. "You may think that I am your problem. That is certainly not the case. Perhaps it would be better to figure out the real reasons why you don't want to _____ (fill in the blank). I would be glad to help with that, if you would like."

Do not allow yourself to be defined as the problem. You can help him to own up to his anxieties, avoidance, and denials. That is in your interest as well as his.

Size of Steps

Psychological growth has been compared to climbing a ladder. An issue is resolved, a function mastered and it is on to the next step. But some steps may be too large for a child to take. The resistance can be dissolved by scaling down the size of the step. Two little steps will carry one further than one large step that is too big to take.

There is a level at which the child can succeed. It is the function of the growth parent to find that level and the size of the steps to be taken. She is then able to encourage the child to accept the challenge of growing beyond the point of resistance. The process of getting from A to B can be kept positive by realizing that a child's hesitancy may result from his impression that the steps are too large; more than he is willing to risk. Some children can get from A to B in one step. Others may require two, three, or more steps to get there. If such a child is expected to get there in one step, he may get nowhere at all.

A common experience illustrates the point. Consider the process by which a child who is confined to the safety of the backyard gains the ability to safely cross the busiest street in town. The process begins at the corner of a street in which the likelihood of a car passing is rather remote. Escorted by his parent, hand in hand, the street is crossed with the child instructed to look one way and then the other. With this skill mastered, the child is then given the opportunity to cross on his own, under the watchful eye of his parent. He soon develops sufficient proficiency to graduate to a busier street. By this time he has developed the habit of looking before leaping, as well as the ability to inhibit the leap should a car be approaching. With more experience, he develops the judgment to time his crossing so that he gets to the other side before an approaching car reaches the intersection. His parent gains confidence that he has mastered the basics and she is willing to allow him to cross the busier streets. He is now free to roam on his own, his growth in this matter has reached the highest levels.

Crossing the street is a metaphor for every type of growth dimension. A shy child may be terrified to separate from his mother. The thought of spending hours in a day care may be more than he can bear. Every experience of separation begins to signal a panic that leads to embarrassing temper tantrums as he attempts to hold onto his parent. Such a child, was brought into my office because she had been expelled from day-care and her mother was perplexed by her daughter's need to grasp onto her.

> Sherri was the most petite and fragile child that I have ever treated. She was matched in size and hair style by her mother. Sherri refused to come in by herself and she insisted on sharing a chair with her mother. No effort was initially made to pry them apart. That would have been a step that was more than Sherri was then able to tolerate. She showed no interest in me, every effort to contact her was summarily rejected.

> Her interest was captured by the games I played at the doll house, fantasy play with the theme of separation. Within a few sessions, Sherri was able to join me in this play. She became sufficiently comfortable with me that I was able to suggest that her mother spend part of the next session in the waiting room, which had a wall in

common with the playroom. Predictably, the suggestion elicited a panic attack in Sherri that dismayed her mother. Nevertheless, I remained firm, letting Sherri know that I was confident she would do just fine. The first part of the ensuing session was spent reassuring Sherri and her apprehensive mother that the time for separation was now at hand. Sherri needed to be restrained from following her mother out the door. The child was quite distraught, but she soon became interested in joining me sending tapping signals to her mother in the adjoining room. This developed into a fun game.

Several sessions later, Sherri was ready to play hide-and-seek throughout the office building. The game began with me hiding and Sherri and her mother trying to find me. Then it was mother who hid, and then Sherri. In our final session, Sherri accompanied me on a three block walk to the local donut shop. We brought one back for her mother, but by that time it was not an important matter to Sherri. Several months later, her father told me that Sherri was back in day-care and was doing fine.

Sherri illustrates the graduated approach to mastering an issue in development. No doubt there are children who can separate and spend lengthy periods away from parents without difficulty. But Sherri required that the steps be scaled down to a size small enough to enable her to take the risks inherent in growth. For children like Sherri, the axioms of the Peter Principle apply. One grows psychologically to the level of incompetence and from that point, growth is resisted. The resistance to growth encompasses fears of loneliness, failure, rejection, and humiliation overwhelming that part of the personality that really wants to grow. The resistance is manifested by withdrawal, avoidance, rebellion, and defiance, behavioral characteristics that obscure the nature of the real problem and entrap parents in fruitless conflicts to which their authority is committed.

A parent who can align herself with that growth-striving part of the child can present a very powerful appeal much more effectively than the parent who attempts an authority solution. Most issues between parent and child lend themselves to the growth perspective analysis. This provides a general strategy whereby avenues can be devised to guide responses that enhance growth.

What Goes Around, Comes Around

Sometimes the battle between a child and parent invades almost every area their relationship. It often seems that a personal vendetta is being played out.

> The battle between twelve year old Jeanine and Mom was violent. She responded to Mom's shove with a punch to the stomach and another to the mouth. Mom was bloodied by the assault. When asked later if she had feelings when she saw her mother bleeding, Jeanine replied, "No, why should I."

> The older of two children of divorce, abandoned by their father, Jeanine had written off the adult world. She felt neglected by her working mother, rejected by an unreliable father. As a young child, she vented her anger by scapegoating her younger sister. When Mother intervened, she was accused of favoring the sister. Sullen, bitter, and defiant, Jeanine had aligned herself with alienated peers. Their behavior mocked adult standards. Sexual promiscuity, truancy, substance abuse, and curfew violations characterized their lifestyles. Several in her group were psychologically disturbed and suicidal. Others were on probation. Jeanine was enraged by her mother's attempts to control and structure her life.

"Where do you get the right to come into my life now
and tell me what to do. You were never there for me
when I really needed you. I don't need you now."

Jeanine's accusation, even if not entirely true, made a telling point. She was accusing Mother of failing to commit
sufficient time and ego to serve her needs and to forge a
meaningful relationship. That is how she saw it and the
facts of the case suggest a reality basis for her view. In her
mind, Mother had relinquished the right to assert parental authority. She had been written off.

———

David was a neonate when his Navy father was assigned
to sea duty. When he returned eight months later, his son
would not respond to him. Subsequently, he was unable
to establish a parental relationship with David. The child
would habitually run to Mom to validate or counter-
mand what his father had asked. Father felt discounted
by his son and unsupported by his wife. But it wasn't that
she was undermining her husband. The son simply could
not apprehend that his father was a coparent. He was a
male relative living in the house.

These cases illustrate how delicate the process is of forg-
ing parental ties to a child. Physical or psychological absence can create a void that is difficult to fill. In these
cases, life circumstances interfered with a parent's ability
to make the commitments. Illness and depression can also
impede the process. Jeanine filled the void with a dysfunctional peer culture. It remains to be seen how David
copes with his void in adolescence. Perhaps, his early experiences with Mom will help him through. His situation is
more wholesome than is Jeanine's.

Centers of Influence

Parents are not included in most growth experiences. Schoolrooms, playgrounds, backyards, the streets are the natural habitats for a child and adolescent. Behavior is guided by what is in the psyche. Decisions, judgments, and standards are the guiding elements of the Adult Ideal. To survive, it is necessary to have the strength to avoid temptation, bad influences, and the pressure to do what is not wholesome. As a child grows, the opportunity for freedom and independence increases. He is on his own, guided by what is in his head. What is it, and how did it get there?

Parents are in the best position to guide the development of the Adult Ideal. Just by being there in meaningful ways and exhibiting attractive qualities, their impact will be strong. They can also shape development by exerting control and access over other potential influences. The power of this is illustrated by the example of religious sects who model appropriate behavior and severely limit unwanted access. They are highly successful in socializing their children to conform to their values and ways.

Parents are less available than ever. Working parents are reliant on surrogates to provide hands-on parenting. Their children are exposed to peers from an early age and they spend an inordinate amount of time in front of television sets. Latchkey children are unsupervised. They seek out others or plant themselves in front of computer screens or television sets viewing behavior that most parents abhor. These experiences influence children in profound ways. It is ironic that television and computer game moguls deny that these programs affect children. Yet, advertisers spend millions of dollars in the media to manipulate children to buy their products. Of course the programs impact children. Their values often conflict with those of a parent. Television is a fox in the chicken coop. A parent has an obligation to eliminate negative influences impinging on her child.

No issues generate more heat than controversies over friends. This is particularly volatile in adolescence. Peers exert enormous influence, while that of the parent begins to wane. Normal adolescent development involves a quest for identity and for psychological emancipation. Friendships are important aspects of the process. The choice of friends that are abhorrent to parents can have several meanings. They could represent a rejection of parental values, ventures into new experiences, assertions of power and freedom, paybacks for past grievances or parental shortcomings. It may not be bad, and yet, it may. Parents are wiser, more experienced. We can generally spot trouble on the horizon. We know the consequences for poor choices can be devastating. The adolescent couldn't care less. We are in a bind because we know that growth is a matter of choice. We also know that our adolescent's choices can be disastrous. We cannot renege on our responsibility. Yet, if the approach is wrong, the effort can backfire.

The parent's position is enhanced with a reservoir of good will that stems from childhood. The adolescent is more likely to assume the legitimacy of his parent's intervention. As we learned from Jeanine, that is not always a given. The seeds of alienation in adolescence are sown in childhood. Parents, be forewarned.

Regardless of position, a parent is advised to avoid placing herself between the adolescent and the friend, no matter how damaging the friendship may be. The "hard line" approach is likely to perpetuate the disharmony and accomplish little. It is always better to emphasize the natural consequences. "I know you believe your friend is a great guy. But I notice that since the two of you began hanging out, your grades have dropped, your life is disorganized, and you have been kicked off the team. Surely, that is not what you want. Isn't it time to reassess what is going on?"

This approach confronts the adolescent with himself, not with you. He may continue to rationalize and deny. But you have left the door open to continue the dialogue and to exert influence. If you see your adolescent as essentially wholesome, you must keep the faith that he will undo bad choices before it is too late. If he is not growing wholesomely, it will not matter.

Chapter 6

Adversity From Without

As parents, many of us dream about the past, about what families are supposed to be. But we cannot quite remember what we dreamed. . . .
　　　　　　　Richard Louv, *Childhood's Future*, 1990

Adversity intrudes as unwelcome events potentially damaging to our psychological growth. The fortunate majority do not experience such disturbances. Their normal development depends on the continuity of a secure, stable family environment.

Maladjustment is often associated with adversity. Because it deviates from the circumstances necessary for normal development it is a hindrance to growth. Conditions in opposition to the normal flow result in warps and obstacles. For example, if continuous relationships with loving parents support wholesome growth, the interruption of relationships through divorce, abandonment, or death impede it.

The reasons are well known. Years of research document the damage generated by adverse circumstances. Typically, children of adversity exhibit more psychological difficulty than other children. Clearly, health is better than illness, stability is preferable to chaos, mature cognitive development beats learning disability, and intact loving families offer more than overwhelmed single-parent families. As a friend observed, "it is much better to be rich, healthy and happy than poor, sick, and miserable."

Granted. No right minded person rejoices at the misfortunes of others. But to view adversity as an unusual event in the lives of only the unfortunate few, to assume that it is inherently and irrevocably damaging, and to overlook its strengthening potential is misleading. The psychology of victimization is an outgrowth of the view that normal development is a product of a limited set of benign conditions and adversity stunts individual psychological growth.

Poverty, racism, loss of a parent, abuse, chronic illness, learning disability, and divorce are facts of life. Millions of children are impacted by these disadvantages, often to their detriment. For many, the challenge is too great to overcome, and they are defeated. Depression, emotional arrest, school drop-outs, and violence speak to the negative power of adversity. But not everyone is so impacted. Some may be damaged in one area while strengthened in another. Determination to overcome may be strengthened in some. While children are vulnerable, they are also adaptable and resilient. Inner vitality and support from others carry some children beyond the limitations of their circumstances. Not only do they survive, but many excel.

In small doses, adversity can have beneficial results. Its function is to help us develop resistance to the stresses of life. Without some adversity, a child remains vulnerable to the tests that will surely come later in life.

Imagine the life of a child with perfect parents who shield him from adversity. Parental perfection denies children the opportunity to appreciate the needs of others, discover strength to survive the world's unfairness or insensitivity, and tolerate disappointment and frustration. Likewise, the child who has it all and whose life appears perfect in all dimensions is deprived. To know only success and acceptance inhibits growth. Rejection, failure, loss, and disappointment, though painful, can strengthen character.

Some children peak too early. Because of extraordinary natural gifts in athletics, physical beauty, and intelligence they are admired, courted, and sometimes exploited. Their lives are narrowed in the service of refining these assets. Time invested is unavailable for developing other aspects of the self. The inability to deal with such advantages is as damaging to growth as adversity. Examples of warped movie stars and chess prodigies, tennis brats, and strikingly beautiful but emotionally troubled people attest to the adversity of too much, too soon.

Large doses of adversity challenge the spirit and increase the prospect of harmful consequences. Trauma and crisis divert children from the business of growing up. Matters of trust, nurturance, and security cannot be taken for granted. If children are subjected to abuse, neglect, and non-supportive environments, their attention is diverted from psychological growth. Management of threat then defines the meaning of life. Childhood has ended.

Children contending with deprivation, abuse, illness, and death are cheated. Worry and manipulation replace playfulness and spontaneity. Survivors of childhood abuse recount grim and terrifying experiences. Chronically ill children contend with pain, stigma, and fear of death. Children of divorce grapple with confused and ambivalent feelings. Danger lurks on the mean streets and in some neighborhood school yards. Survival should not be the issue of growth and development.

These are not anomalies. To take the view that adversity is inherently and irrevocably damaging commits generations of children to bleak and ungratifying futures. A society in irreversible decline is the only outcome. Adversity predisposes but does not condemn children to damage. In individual cases, children survive, transcend, and are strengthened by adversity. The worst predictions of the experts do not always come true. Damaging events may not damage. Vulnerable children may deflect threats and defeat adversity.

> Baby Jessica, taken from her adoptive parents with whom she had lived for the first years of her life, was returned to her birth parents. Emotional bonds were severed and the separation was difficult. The disruption is likely to make future emotional investments difficult. Yet, Jessica attached to her biological parents and appears to be a happy, normally developed child. It is too early to tell.

It is important to note that experts advised against returning Jessica to her biological parents on the grounds that it was against her best interests. The best interests of the child may not be as clearly discernible as the experts believe.

Larry, a biracial child, was abandoned in the basement of an apartment building by his crack addicted mother. Rescued by Social Services, he was placed with a Caucasian foster family for two years. During this time, his Afro-American great aunt sought his custody. A childless, unmarried woman from a distant state, she felt a family obligation to raise the child. A lengthy legal battle resulted in a change of custody.

Abandonment, removal from caring parents, relocation across the country, racial discontinuity, and placement with an inexperienced single parent constitutes major trauma. Despite dire predictions, Larry is adjusting well. Few problems have surfaced after two years with his aunt. Perhaps his adversity has planted an emotional time bomb to explode later. The possibility that he will function well, however, cannot be discounted. Damaged in some ways, he may be strengthened in others.

Eleanor Roosevelt overcame significant childhood adversity to emerge as a twentieth century icon.

By her eighth year, Eleanor experienced the deaths of her mother and a younger brother. She was emotionally attached to her alcoholic father. Unfit to raise his children, her father, Elliott, was exiled by the family and died when his daughter was ten years old. Her cold and indifferent, maternal grandmother assumed the parenting role. Eleanor grew up in lonely and emotionally impoverished circumstances.

Eleanor always considered her father her most important influence. Despite his serious deficiencies, he instilled a noble vision that guided her throughout life. It enabled her to empathize with and advocate for those in need. Her boundless caring and humanity blossomed from the seeds of a suffering childhood. Personal emotional scarring impacted her private life. But the strengthening aspects of adversity led her to greatness.

Of course, we cannot be Eleanor Roosevelt. Her intelligence, privileged social status, and membership in the Teddy Roosevelt clan were advantages. As first lady, she could champion causes and be heard. But also important to her ability to transcend adversity was the influence of a teacher who recognized her abilities and encouraged Eleanor to discover her self-worth. This is an influence that may be possible to all of us.

The experience of Eleanor illustrates the importance of adult influence. The growth perspective maintains that the Adult Ideal gives direction to growth striving. It also requires confidence to take the emotional risks that promote growth and her teacher was important in this regard. Her father provided a vision, her teacher, an inspiration. Eleanor's experience provides a framework for understanding the value of adults in helping children cope with adversity.

Vision and inspiration introduce possibilities unknown to children. These deeper qualities give meaning to children in crisis. Sharing pain, providing perspective and comfort in time of need are natural adult responses to those who are suffering. Yet, as important as these parenting qualities are, they are often suppressed in the rush of daily life. A harried parent is more concerned with discipline and supervision. Responding to an emergency negates concern about a messy room. Resolve the emergency and the mess becomes the focus of interaction.

One can ponder Elliott Roosevelt's impact on Eleanor had he the emotional capacity to be her custodial parent. Would the vision he provided be blurred in battles over cleaning the dishes? This does not suggest that orderliness and responsibility should be ignored. It reminds parents that what is given to children during times of emergency can also be given in mundane, every day living, even though the child is likely to be less receptive. Emergencies reorder priorities. What was important becomes trivial. A parent, taken for granted, is better appreciated.

The qualities that emerge are incorporated into the developing Adult Ideal, broadening and deepening the child's understanding of adulthood's potential. What emerges from adversity and is maintained during ordinary times, appeals to a child's courage, helps him rise to the occasion and models the essence of maturity. This silver lining is hidden within the dark clouds of adversity and is lost in the fog of daily living. Many children and their parents, groping through the dark, lose the way. The silver lining is an important beacon to seek and follow.

Surviving adversity does not mean that emotional damage is completely resolved. It means that its impact increases rather than limits personality growth. Like Eleanor Roosevelt, children of adversity, with the help of adults, can translate losses and pain into appreciation of their strengths, compassion for others, and increased determination to make the most out of life. Many advocates of good causes are motivated by what they gained from earlier adverse experiences. Altruism expresses the best emerging from experiencing the worst.

Adversity is part of the human condition. Within its pain and sadness are opportunities to facilitate growth. This is a difficult challenge for children and their parents. The following sections examine some common forms of adversity for children and describe the experiences of children, maladaptive coping tendencies, pitfalls for parents, and possible avenues of solution.

Divorce

It is the context in which divorce occurs that determines whether separation and divorce adversely affect child development.
William F. Hodges,
Interventions for Children of Divorce, 1986

Unhappy marriage presents a crucial test of parenthood values. The dilemma is to resolve the issue of marital unhappiness while protecting the interest of the children. While acknowledging that their marriage was the result of mistaken judgment, many parents are unwilling to live with its consequences. Divorce is the logical solution, occurring at the rate of about one million per year.

Many relationships cannot be fixed. The best, and only solution to unfixable and personally destructive relationships, is divorce. These are relationships that are physically threatening, emotionally stifling, completely incompatible, utterly unbearable, totaling enmeshing, lacking in rapport, and absurdly improbable. Suffering abuse, losing dignity, bearing dishonesty is too high a personal price to sustain any relationship. The decision to divorce acknowledges that remedy is not possible—the ungratifying and destructive patterns of interaction are so rigid wholesome change cannot occur.

Yet, the consequences of divorce can be detrimental to children. It shatters the rhythms of life that had been established and sets in motion new parameters for living. Children are required to adjust to circumstances in which their interests are peripheral.

Five year old Carla lives with Mom. She is distraught when Dad arrives for his alternate weekend visits. Carla worries and obsesses about Mom. She cannot sleep. Dad is frustrated and dismayed that his daughter is unable to enjoy the visit.

———

Eight year old Ricky loves to play soccer. His team plays on Saturday when Ricky is with Dad, fifty miles away. When Dad won't drive, Ricky can't play. A solution is found. Ricky practices during the week with the team near Mom's house. He plays on Saturday with a team in Dad's town. "I feel like a basketball," confides Ricky.

———

Norman and Ruth have lived with Dad since stepdad abused them. Norman hates Mom and will not visit her. Now twelve years old, he blames Mom for his frustrations and disappointments. His life is a mess and it's Mom's fault.

———

Sixteen year old Carlton lacks the courage to tell Dad that he'd rather be with his friends. Dad has been granted weekend visits. He gets angry when his rights are ignored. His daughter, Melanie, finesses the situation. Fortunately, her suicide attempt fails. But her lengthy hospitalization has upset the visitation routine. A therapist cautions to suspend visits until issues are resolved. Dad is invited, but refuses to attend family meetings. Melanie is delighted to spend weekends at home.

———

Brooke and Brandi are young teenagers raised by Dad. He remarries a young and caring woman interested in relating to the girls. Brooke and Brandi are determined to destroy the marriage. They do. In the process, their outrageous behavior costs them the chance to grow. More time is spent in juveniles hall than in study hall. Drugs, sex, truancy, runaways, psychiatric hospitalization are the lifestyle. The turmoil lasts for years.

——

Timmy informs Mom that there will be war if she marries Warren. She does and there is. Taxed to her limit, Mom seeks relief by placing Timmy in temporary foster care. Weekend visits are proceeding nicely. One Friday, before a scheduled visit, ten year old Timmy is found dead, hanging from a tree. The police are unable to determine whether an accident or suicide is the cause of death.

Children of divorce are diverted from normal development to issues dealing with the dissolution of the family. Divorce introduces overwhelming adversity into the lives of many children. Some rise to the occasion and gain strength from coping with the stresses. Others suffer temporarily and then resume the business of growing up. Many are damaged in important and lasting ways. Unhappy marriage is not in the interest of children. Neither is divorce. That should be the last, not the first, recourse to an unhappy marriage.

Many unhappy marriages are not so potentially destructive that dissolution is the best alternative. Remedies within the marriage are possible given motivation and perspective. An attitude that enables distressed couples to value resolution over dissolution, that favors the riskier and more difficult above the easier course of action, is required. The difficulty arises from focusing the need to change upon the self, rather than the other, in order to foster personal growth within the difficult relationship. In contrast, dissolution enables the focus to remain on the shortcomings of the other and to channel emotions into destructive battles. To promote resolution, a commitment from both parties, each focusing on the self rather than the other can salvage a marriage.

When children are part of the family, and the marital problems less than damaging, parents are obliged first to seek solutions within the marriage. There are many advantages for doing so, and divorce remains an option should within-marriage resolution fail. Consider these advantages.

- An adequate within-marriage solution, results when each parent reflects on the real causes of the distress, reassesses values and priorities, realizes that some expectations may be unrealistic, appreciates the other's strengths and finds way of coping with the limitations. Acceptance of the other, for better and for worse, modulates frustration and anger. Stress is reduced with improvement in the emotional life of the family. Resolution on this level results in personal growth. That is worth considerably more than a hefty divorce settlement.

- Within-marriage resolution prevents an emotionally and financially draining divorce process. A divorce upheaval can endure for years. Divorce may solve some problems and create others. It may not work for everyone in the family. Everything has a price. Who is paying for this divorce? If the children, is it worth the price? When such questions are asked, one is wrestling with parenthood.

- Divorce is difficult for children. It need not be damaging, but in many cases it is. The anecdotes at the beginning of this section describe the stresses, frustration, diversions, disruptions, and turmoil that frequently enter the lives of children of divorce. Seeking solution for marital problems that prevent such consequences is a tribute to strong parenthood values.

* Within-marriage resolution may fail and divorce is inevitable. Even if the prospects for success are bleak, the attempt should be made. One lives with the consequences of decisions and it is important to know that every effort was made to work things out. That efforts did not pay off is unfortunate. Parents and children will find it easier to accept the consequences of a failed marriage knowing that a real effort was made to resolve the problems prior to seeking the divorce.

When marriage fails, parents are then obliged to be coping resources for their children. Studies show that among the important factors leading to successful outcome are the ability of parents to support each other, set aside differences, and communicate reasonably. Divorce dissolves marriage, not the coparenting relationship. A redefinition of this relationship on behalf of the children is required. The process is complicated when parents neither like nor respect the other, remain unresolved over property or money, or divorce agreements are unhonored. It is difficult to close the chapter on an unhappy marriage when disharmony impedes the coparenting relationship. Divorce does not wish away the other, even though the temptation to do so is great. Despite negative feelings, high levels of frustration, or contempt, parents are obliged to work toward harmonious relations. It is in the interest of the children to do so.

Visitation

Visitation is an issue that tests the mettle of parents and the maturity of children. Experts agree that children benefit from access to each parent. Arrangements typically ensure a primary residence and significant visitation with the non-custodial parent. Complications can develop from the most basic matters.

The Exchange

Exchanges require interactions between parents. One enters the territory of the other. The nature of contact varies from cordiality to complete avoidance. Children are sensitive to the subtle messages communicated by their parents. These can be calming and reassuring or anxiety provoking. Children are relieved by experiencing a relaxed exchange.

Transition

It is difficult to transition between environments. No one likes to live out of a suitcase, but visitation requires children to do so. The rules, conditions, and emotional atmosphere in each home may be substantially different. Confusion and feelings of alienation may result.

Seven year old Bonnie was troubled by twelve year old David calling her father "Dad." David, the son of Dad's new wife had more contact with her father than she did. Bonnie felt betrayed and replaced. She resented that Dad loved David as much as her.

Unfamiliar noises and shadows, the absence of comforting pets, differences in food preparation, are small matters that can be upsetting to young children. Awareness of the little things can help parents to reassure a visiting child.

Competing Agendas

As children grow their lives become more and more centered out of home. Friends, sports, and mastery activities capture interest and become primary agendas. Visitation may compete with these. While desiring a relationship with the non-custodial parent, many children resent doing so should it deprive them of opportunity to follow their agenda. Judges, lawyers, and parents, not the children, construct the visitation schedule. Formulas based on preconceived notions, not the preferences of children, determine visitation. It is important to respect the preferences of the children. Rarely, in an intact family will children choose to spend weekends with parents if there are better things to do. So to with visitation. To the extent that visitation is integrated with children's agendas, to that extent will it be harmonious.

Divided Loyalty
It is difficult to enjoy Dad's company or to accept a stepmom should a child sense that Mom is still angry. It is disloyal to enjoy the visit. He relates only the negative. Mom's anger is validated and intensified. The child aligns himself with her anger to protect his relationship with her.

Children are not served by taking sides. They need both parents to shield them from resentment. Children will form their own judgments. If Dad doesn't care, they will find out soon enough. They may also find that while he failed as a spouse, he can succeed as a parent.

Secret Wishes

No matter how improbable, many children believe that their parents will reconcile. Despite remarriage or other reality factors, the wish is maintained. It operates in a way that make it difficult or impossible to accept new realities. Problems with step-parenting or adjustment to single parenting may be intensified by the secret wish for reconciliation. Resolution is impeded by the conflict between wish and reality. Unacknowledged tension may fuel inappropriate behavior that aims to clear away obstacles to reconciliation. The psychological dynamics can be quite complex, with many variations on the theme. It is difficult to decipher the meaning of the child's behavior. Professional assistance may be necessary to clarify issues and keep matters under control.

Role Reversal

Many children assume responsibility for the well-being of their parents. They worry about Mom while visiting Dad. She may be lonely or in danger. They also worry that Mom may enjoy her free time; that she will forget them. Children may want to protect the parent from conflict or anger. They withhold troublesome information. On the other hand, they reveal upsetting news or behave in ways that require Mom's time and energy. Mixed messages, competing tendencies, hidden anxieties can make life exhausting.

Reality Versus Fantasy

The frustrations of life with the custodial parent can be transformed into fantasy that with the other parent it would be better. Children of divorce confront the harsh realities of parental unavailability, loneliness, increased responsibility, conflict with the custodial parent, feeling they are no longer important. All these problems would be resolved, so they fantasize, were they with the other parent. A bleak reality cannot compete with such a fantasy. Indeed, it serves to heighten the frustration and alienation. In my experience, changes in custody do not necessarily solve such problems. It is better that parents support each other to address their child's concerns.

The major challenge for parents who choose divorce as the solution to unhappy marriage is to set aside differences, assume goodwill, provide support, communicate well, resolve differences in a reasonable way. These are the best avenues for maximizing the prospects for children. Divorce serves the interest of one or both parents, but not necessarily children. Divorced parents can give them no better gift than a positive coparenting relationship.

The Family in Transition

> *We are in the midst of defining divorce as an enduring societal institution much in the same way as we have viewed marriage in our culture.*
>
> Constance R. Ahrons and Roy H. Rodgers,
> *Divorced Families*, 1987

Divorce, death, and out-of-wedlock births change the context of child rearing. These conditions introduce major stresses and discontinuities into the lives of children. The events and the need to restructure are unsettling and confusing.

The growth perspective seeks opportunities for growth in the face of adversity. But it also recognizes that undue stresses can be detrimental. The problems of reconstructed or non-traditional families can be emotionally, socially, and financially overwhelming. Coping with losses, mixed loyalties, new family alignments, rivalries, and general instability are immense challenges. Brief discussions follow of some of the issues facing children in families structured in non-traditional ways.

The Reconstructed Family (simple type)

A family consisting of a parent, step-parent, and any number of siblings, step-siblings and half-siblings is a simple reconstructed family. This common arrangement typically results from divorce and remarriage. On a structural level, the form emulates a traditional two-parent family, with one or two working parents. To the extent that remarriage solves the conflicts and disharmony in the family, improvement in the psychological climate is likely.

However, there are several areas of emotional complication in this arrangement. Often, the emotional aftermath of divorce colors the way a step-parent can be accepted. The very fact of remarriage conflicts with the inner child's wish that parents will be reunited. Accepting the new parent creates loyalty conflict and demolishes the wish for reconciliation. The attitudes of the non-custodial parent, in support of or opposition to the reconstructed family, can be a factor. Withholding financial support intensifies conflicts to the detriment of the child. In addition, relationships with step and half-siblings can aggravate the situation. Problems may also arise from the simple fact that the child maintains a surname different from others in the reconstructed family. Part-time parenting may present problems. The immensity of the emotional challenge facing people in reconstructed families is increased when there is only time and energy to parent part-time.

The Reconstructed Family (complex type)

This consists of two sets of parents, step-parents, and an assortment of sibling relationships. It derives from divorce settlements giving each parent significant contact with the child. Joint custody or informal arrangements develop in this family structure. It is typically set-up on a time-sharing schedule. The child literally belongs to two households, with permanent living space in each. Some families live in close proximity, so that changing households does not require changing schools and friends. In other situations, it means exactly that. The child is split in a manner that Solomon would not have allowed.

This arrangement can work on behalf of the child only if there is a reservoir of goodwill between the parents and a commonality in terms of values, attitudes, and discipline. It also helps if the child feels acceptance from each stepparent. For without that, the child is likely to feel more a visitor than a member of either household. The delicacy of this arrangement is apparent. Under the best of circumstances, the child can benefit from the increase of people who are interested in his welfare and want to be important influences in his life. In circumstances that are less then the best, the child is subjected to conflict, stress, mixed loyalties, manipulations, and emotional entrapment.

Single Parenting

The one parent family may derive from divorce, out-of-wedlock birth, or death of a parent. This kind of family structure implies a history of discontinuity or disruption in the lives of the parent and/or the child. The emotional issues are highly complex, regardless of the actual derivation of the family. The structural weaknesses of the single-parent family are all too evident.

Typically, the single parent assumes the roles of primary breadwinner and parent/homemaker. Her financial status is likely to be insecure and her standard of living considerably below that of the intact family. In many cases, emotional support is quite limited. She may be geographically as well as psychologically alienated from extended family. She encounters many obstacles in her attempt to recruit adequate surrogates.

Some women consider single parenting to be temporary. Social needs may compete with the child's needs for parenting. Should a significant other be brought into the household, the relationship of her child to this person may generate stress and insecurity rather than support. For the child is likely to be more needy and dependent than the intact-family child. Twice the emotional neediness with half the parental availability creates a highly intense emotional situation. Only the most emotionally mature, energetic, and creative of persons can manage the challenges of single parenting. The sad fact is that many single parents are the least mature, emotionally, and financially able to care for children. Where maximum support is needed, minimum support is available.

There is no adequate societal response to the needs of the single parent. No guiding model beyond the weak emulation of the traditional family sustains the increasing numbers of one parent families, mostly headed by females. The minority of single parent fathers face similar stresses and challenges. Innovative approaches in dealing with the single parent family are needed.

Unready or Ill-equipped Parents

Stephen: What have you got against having children?
Simon: Well Steve, in the first place there isn't enough room.
. . . and in the sixth place I don't like them very much in the first place. OK.
        Simon Gray, *Otherwise Engaged*, 1975, Act III

Sometimes it seems that a child has not had a chance from the moment of conception.

Steve, a murderer, was sentenced to die for senselessly killing two people in a series of gas station robberies. These were not the only lives he had taken.

This nineteen year old had been conceived to a young
woman out-of-wedlock whose religious beliefs prevented
her from having an abortion. But they did not prevent
her from abandoning her family four years later. The
child was raised by his ex-marine father, who had little interest or ego investment in parenting. The boy was
lonely, neglected, and occasionally sternly disciplined. At
age eleven, he realized that power and respect were accorded to the toughest kids in the school yard. Steve
made a basic existential decision—to be a gangster. Petty
crimes escalated and led to juvenile detention. He committed murder shortly after release.

His mother was asked to attend the trial. She refused. She
believed her son was a danger and better off dead.
Clearly, she was asking the state to perform the abortion
that she was reluctant to have.

A hypothetical but typical suburban high school located
in a middle-class neighborhood has teams of professionals
serving the needs of dysfunctional students. Problems of
truancy, underachievement, pregnancy, suicide, and violence are discussed. Inevitably family problems are uncov-
ered. Usually, single-parent mothers, unsupported by the
fathers, define the family structure with ill-equipped parents.

But even intact families can be made of parents who are
ill-equipped and dysfunctional. There is a high correla-
tion between parenting/parenthood deficiencies and
growth resistance. These are not always unloving or uncaring parents, although some are. But something is clearly
amiss in each case. Their children are surly, arrogant, and
do not want to grow up. The school arranges meetings to
address the problems and to motivate the student.
Teacher, social worker, dean, administrator, counselor,

nurse, and psychologist seek innovative solutions. A grateful parent offers suggestions. More often than not, the student is out to lunch. He sits, passive and unresponsive, as if the meeting has nothing to do with him. He bides his time waiting to be relieved of this ordeal so that he can get on with the real business of hanging out and cutting class with his friends. Should a family issue be addressed, the student is resentful. He turns against his parents, accusing them of controlling him. He is not about to pitch in and help. He conveys the attitude that he is the victim of inadequate parenting and is deserving of restitution. He is insulted that he is asked to pitch in, and to grow up. The parents are inadequate in this child's eyes.

These are not the problems of a misguided few. Conservatively, fifteen percent of the student body is identified as "at risk." Their readiness to function adequately as adults is dubious. They reject high school as an opportunity to help them get ready. What other opportunities will they have?

From the growth perspective, these teenagers have failed to develop a mature and functional Adult Ideal. They lack a vision and the confidence to strive toward wholesome goals. The parents have obviously exhibited qualities that are not acceptable to their children. The breadwinning, unsupported single parent has needs of her own. She is not emotionally available to her needy child. He perceives her as mean, demanding, and uncaring. He has no sympathy for her efforts. Absentee father is idealized or despised. He does not come through when needed. Why would the child identify with his parents?

Neil Postman wrote in *The Disappearance of Childhood* "the adult-child may be defined as a grown-up whose intellectual and emotional capacities are unrealized and, in particular, not significantly different from those associated with children."* He reports further that this was the norm in the Middle Ages and that he believes that the adult-child is emerging as normal at the present time.

Are there solutions for children or adolescents raised by unready or ill-equipped parents, validated by like-minded peers, and influenced by media that projects highly immature behavior as adult behavior?

While the prospects for children and adolescents in such circumstances seems bleak, it is not a completely hopeless situation. An alienated teenager may decide that, unlike his older peers, he did not want to spend his life flipping hamburgers. Others have accepted influence from adults other than parents. Still others have reached into themselves and discovered talents and strengths not previously known. Once the natural consequences of their attitudes and behaviors become apparent, many adolescents reassess their lives and find means for turning them around. Whether the norm or the exception, it is hard to know. Neil Postman presents the pessimistic view.

Parents are urged not to give up on their alienated, rebellious children and adolescents. Although they have been "fired" from their roles of guide, mentor, monitor, supervisor, and enforcer they can yet contribute to the welfare and growth of their offspring. They can exert influence in more subtle and indirect ways. This requires that they redefine themselves as parents. For what they have been doing is not working. A parent cannot easily relinquish her protective, caring, and supervisory responsibilities. But

*Postman, Neil, *The Disappearance of Childhood*, (New York: Vintage Books, 1994), 99.

neither can she pretend that she is ready and equipped if she is not. It is important that she is honest and admit to her inadequacies. For some, counseling or parent support groups can help. Others enlist support from relatives, neighbors, or friends. Some community programs may be available, but realistically, few programs can replace parental involvement. At best, these are stop-gap measures. The parent is obliged to do the best that she can do to keep her child in the ball game, enlist as much assistance as available, and be there for her child.

Ill-equipped parents of adolescents are in a bind. Their ability to influence is likely to be minimal, yet they cannot responsibly ignore his poor choices. The rebellious teenager is unlikely to conform his behavior to the expectations of his parent. There is no point in engaging in authority battles that accomplish little more than generating tension and ill will.

There are some parents who literally "divorce" contentious teenagers. They provide food, shelter, and clothing. They insulate themselves as best they can from the irresponsible behavior of the teenager. The natural consequences of this behavior inevitably attracts the attention of the authorities. The less recalcitrant adolescents are sometimes able to conform under threats of legal entanglements. Others respond to tracker programs administered by probation departments. Trackers provide intense supervision. They see that the teenager is up in the morning, gets to school, and finds a job. They have the authority to recommend placement should the adolescent resist. In some cases, trackers form positive alliances with their charges and serve as role models.

Although parental authority has shifted to the public authorities, parents still have a role in the lives of their off-spring. While they may be unready and ill-equipped as parents, they may make terrific surrogate aunts or uncles. Traditionally, aunts and uncles can be involved, special, and influential. While out of the direct line of authority, they can support, counsel, and commit intimate time to the adolescent. A parent may be a lousy disciplinarian and inadequate caretaker but a loving, concerned adult. Just because she has relinquished authority doesn't mean that she is unable to contribute in important ways.

Not only teenagers, but many adults are unready and ill-equipped to raise children. The temperamentally un-suited, those unable to commit time or ego, those who do not like children, or are unable to sustain gratifying relations are likely to be poor parents.

Those who are sexually active or want to procreate are advised to assess their readiness to be a parent. They court personal disaster should they bring a child into the world without the means to provide for its welfare and growth.

The measures that were described above are only band-aids. Neither parent nor child can thrive unless the timing and readiness are appropriate. Unready or ill-equipped parents do a disservice to themselves as well as to their children.

Individuals who understand and accept their shortcomings for parenthood are to be congratulated for choosing not to have children. Indeed, why not accord them honor? To Mother's Day in May and Father's Day in June add Non-parent's Day in July. Why not a Non-parent of the Year Award? Surely the recipient of such an award is contributing more to society than an ill-equipped parent.

This idea may not be popular or politically correct but survival of our culture is at stake.

Latchkey Children

Going home becomes an excursion into isolation, or (from a teenager's point of view) into a child's wonderland, a separate world free of adult restrictions.

Richard Louv, *Childhood's Future*, 1990

Many children raise themselves in bleak, lonely circumstances. Lacking initiative, self-sufficiency, and ingenuity, they care for themselves. They are instructed to remain in the house, without companions, until a parent returns. Trapped in an empty house for upwards of several hours, they vegetate. Many evolve into couch potatoes watching reruns or contemporary soap operas graphically depicting casual sexual encounters, drugs, and violence. Nintendo addicts can hardly be pried from the control apparatus. The more socially adept monopolize the telephone. It is a rare latchkey child who completes a homework assignment, reads a book, or develops a creative project.

Older and more defiant children disobey the rules. They do not immediately come home from school. Their lives are mysteries to parents skeptical of the explanations. Where did they really go? They cannot confirm that an adult was present and the activity innocent. Conflict and distrust are generated by parents' inability to supervise *in absentia*. Children reject the absent adult, adopt each other for support, affirmation, and excitement. Activities may include gang membership, substance abuse groupies, dungeon and dragons cliques, or unsafe sexual activities. Children without social skills remain withdrawn and isolated, and may be subject to depression.

After school programs available to children and adolescents lack appeal to many. The babysitter is repugnant. Extended day programs generate fatigue and conflict. Activities, clubs, sports programs, and scouts are uninteresting or involve logistical problems that render them useless. Children have had enough and they want to go home.

The more vital children welcome the independence. They participate in their world with competence and excitement. Skills are mastered, imagination stimulated, social life enhanced, and time structured wholesomely. A long day away from parents and home is tolerable. For such children latchkey status enhances growth striving.

Parents recognizing the need to spend more time with their children may feel ignored at home. Children prefer to be with friends, hog the telephone, or withdraw into the sanctuary of the bedroom. Closed doors, music, and computers create barriers that parents cannot penetrate. Children are not home to interact with a parent, although they may do so if there is nothing better to do or if they need a favor. It may seem to parents that their presence is irrelevant.

The difference between isolation from a parent and being home alone is substantial, but it is not in how the parental presence affects the child's reality. For in many instances, an absent parent has arranged experiences that offer much more than does being at home.

Companionship, stimulation, and nurturance come with the planned program. By objective standards, a child should welcome and thrive in these situations. However, a child's reactions may be determined by other factors, and the child may prefer home to supervised programs. The child may complain of boredom, peer conflict and indifferent authority. A playmate accepted at home is rejected in day care. What is boring with a babysitter is enjoyable at home.

The child's point of view is important. Children have histories and temperaments that determine their responses to latchkey status. It may represent a discontinuity or a crisis in their life. Some children are born to be cared for by surrogates. Maternal leave enables a mother three to six months to provide hands-on parenting. When she returns to the work force, the care of the child is assigned to others. That event is postponed for children whose mother chooses to stay home until the children enter preschool or kindergarten.

Divorce impels dramatic shifts in circumstances for many children. Along with the loss of one parent, the other parent who may have chosen to provide hands-on parenting now returns to the work force. A change in neighborhood, school, and economic conditions accompany the transition to latchkey status. For some the triggering event is the death of a parent. The issues associated with loss are rejection, betrayal, grief, and insecurity. The child's world view is shattered. He may feel less important than was previously believed. Such feelings can emerge in two parent families as well. A child perceives that the parent's wage earning activity is more important than he.

By ages ten to twelve, many children develop resistance to after care. The urge for independence is strong but readiness lacking. A parent is pressured to acquiesce. When all else fails, a child gets expelled from the program. Ready or not, he is on his own.

Sensing a lack of parental investment, the child responds in kind. Growth resistance emerges in reaction to latch-key conditions. Emptiness mirrors the inner feelings of the child. Parents often attempt to fill the void with chores and suggestions that homework should be completed by a certain time each day. As reasonable as it seems to the parent, the demands and suggestions are ignored by the child. His time is spent passively eating and and watching television. Mom is not available to care for his needs, reasons the child, but she is asking him to care for her needs. How the child will fill the time becomes a battleground of conflict. Mom's sense of guilt and junior's resentment and feelings of deprivation are obscured. The conflict does not solve any problem but instead fosters alienation and provides a basis for rejecting parental credibility and value.

The evolving Adult Ideal is impacted. The child perceives harried, demanding, unfair, and humorless adults. It is better to maintain a child's concept of the adult without the unpleasant complications. The emotional qualities of the child and his ideas of adulthood are perpetuated, causing a slowdown in emotional development. The media, to which the child has turned to fill the emptiness, confirms that arrested development is really adult.

Approaching adolescence, a child develops the freedom and physical capacity to act out the immature concept of adulthood. Like-minded friends validate the attractiveness of the immature Adult Ideal. No longer invested in a relationship with parents, the adolescent is free to invest emotionally in peers. As many gang members have stated, the gang is family. The adult world has lost its influence. Immature activities such as substance abuse, sexual promiscuity, and violence are typical peer norms. The conflict with parental expectations is obvious. But with waning influence and increasing alienation, a parent is unable to interrupt the process.

Latchkey children are a fact of life in today's world. Parents often must join the work place to satisfy economic and ego needs. Good day care and babysitters help with the latchkey problem. However, their value is limited. They provide care, protection, and entertainment, but cannot instill the sense of specialness that is crucial to the emotional well-being of children. This is reserved for the unique parent/child relationship. Only parents with an investment in the child can give this. If circumstances take parents away from ongoing, hands-on relationships as the avenue for instilling specialness, other ways can be found for doing so.

It is unlikely that time diverted from parenting to the work place can be replaced. Homemaking parents instill specialness through the accumulated affect of daily, low impact experience with the child. Working parents can provide higher impact experiences. What is lost in time is recaptured by special events.

My younger son and I were charter members of the Friday Morning Breakfast Club that met on Thursdays. A priority event, it was canceled only for cosmic reasons. With breakfast, we discussed issues and events. It was his exclusive time and, as president, he set the agenda. A temperamental nine year old, he once resigned in anger. I did not accept his resignation. Others, including family members, could attend by invitation only. They were rarely invited. The experience became a highlight of the week.

Years later, when home from college, my son reminded me that the breakfast club had not met in a while. We reconvened and our reminiscing confirmed the importance the club was to him. This high impact experience featured a silly premise (our private joke), exclusivity, and mutual commitment. It compensated for the many times that I was not at the dinner table or was otherwise unavailable to my family.

_____

Peak experiences are remembered for a lifetime. A two-for-one air fare when my son was sixteen years old provided an opportunity to spend a week in San Francisco. The spontaneity and excitement of the event communicated the high value that I placed on our relationship despite the times that unavoidable demands were higher on my agenda.

There are less dramatic ways to communicate the message of specialness to a child. Moments set the tone and timing is important. When arriving home from work, parents can focus on the child and listen with interest. Forget about the chores. That can come later. So can attention to your own needs. No matter how tiring and frustrating your day was, pay attention to the quality of your entry into the home. If you let him know by your manner and actions that you are glad to be home and to see him, the relationship is enhanced. You want your arrival to signal positive anticipation. If the child expects criticism and complaints about unfinished tasks, it will be difficult to generate warmth and good feelings later. Much good can be accomplished by consistently coming through the door with positive feeling.

Constructing a life to compensate for what is lacking is particularly important for single parents without a supportive extended family or social support system. Work and parenting demands are so great that it is difficult to develop a gratifying social life. Often the need for adult relationships competes with a child's needs and expectations.

Single parents can build surrogate families. People with similar needs and lifestyles can complement each other and share burdens and strengths. In alliance, parents become surrogate aunts and uncles to each other's children . A child is given the sense of belonging to a wider network within which he is special. An evening with aunt and cousins has a higher meaning than one with a babysitter.

Friendships with children of a relative add dimension to the quality of life in the family. This provides a coalescing rather than a competition of needs. Shared experiences with other children helps lessen alienation and conflicts with parents.

While latchkey circumstances are not the child-rearing conditions of choice, they increasingly define current reality. Many children lack the maturity to manage well on their own. They are at risk to develop behavioral and emotional problems. These risks are reduced by finding means to compensate for what is lost in time to the work place. The challenge can bring out the best and need not lead to adverse results.

Chapter 7

Adversity From Within

Sweet are the uses of adversity,
Which, like the toad, ugly and venomous,
Wears yet a precious jewel in his head.
            William Shakespeare, *As You Like It*, Act II, 1599

The previous chapter addressed problems of adversity experienced by children due to divorce, single parenting, and other non-traditional family structures.

But, some things having to do with the child and not the physical structure of families have an adverse affect on the psychological growth of a child. It may be a psychological or physical handicap which contributes to a growth problem, and many parents may simply not be up to the job due to immaturity, emotional problems, or a lack of knowledge or desire. It's important for parents to recognize these problems and deal with potential maladjustments. The following sections cover special issues dealing with learning disabilities, adolescence, and childhood asthma.

Learning Disability

. . . no single factor or even set of factors can account for the heterogeneous group of children included in the category of learning or reading disturbance.
Christoph M. Heinakie, *Manual of Child Psychopathology*, 1972

Four major experiences test the hero fantasy and shape unconscious attitudes about growth: fantasy play, sibling relationships, school athletics, and school classrooms.

Growth is promoted if the experiences are favorable. Too many experiences of failure and frustration can lead to growth resistance.

Learning is a product of a neurological system sufficiently developed so that attention is focused, information stored, processed, and retrieved. Motor functions are refined to enable movements needed to express intellectual, speech/language, and writing skills. Cognitive abilities that form discrimination and sequencing precede the development of reading skills. To be emotionally ready for school, a child should be secure and confident. Positive self-esteem enables a child to look forward to, not fear, learning. Good social skills and a positive attitude toward authority enhances the social aspects of schooling.

School programs are devised with the expectation that children five and a half to six years old are ready for school in the learning, motor, cognitive, and social areas. But many are not ready. A child with an immature or damaged nervous system is unable to focus attention, inhibit responses, or control impulses. Such a child is frequently identified as having Attention Deficit Disorder (A.D.D.). Children may be perceptually disorganized or immature in regard to fine motor skills. Some cannot compete, assert themselves, or share with others. Others may need attention, be fatigued, or distrust authority. Learning is difficult for these and other reasons. The child senses school is likely to be a frustrating and unsuccessful experience. Children who are not ready to meet the demands of school are predisposed to develop learning disability (LD).

Inevitable frustration and failure are publicly displayed in the classroom and magnified by negative peer reactions. Many LD children lack balance and coordination and are poor athletes. Here, too, their weaknesses are on public display and subject them to further humiliation.

Often LD children are intellectually bright. Ironically, this can compound the difficulty. For in attempting to make sense of their problems, they conclude that they are stupid. Adults who attempt to correct this distortion are dismissed as merely trying to make them feel better. Their truth is extracted from their pain and humiliation. Resistance to growth is an inevitable consequence.

Maladaptive Coping

Developmental lines that are affected include responsibility and self-sufficiency. Commonly the LD child is adept at transforming growth resistance into authority issues. Parents, abetted by the school, make willing cohorts. LD students are also adept at converting growth resistance into behavior problems. Any problem is better than testing the basic appraisal that he is really stupid.

No labels are as devastating to a child as stupid, dumb, or retarded. It is logical for an LD student to infer that his learning problem is the result of an inborn intellectual deficit. These children go to great lengths to avoid the implication and this leads to many forms of maladaptive coping.

Negative Attitudes Toward Help

Special education programs are available to LD students. But to accept help, one must accept that it is needed. Many LD students have trouble accepting help. Acceptance, to a child, is tantamount to publicly announcing that he is stupid. To avoid this implication he denies that he needs help and rejects attempts to convince him otherwise.

Negative Attitudes Toward Effort

Practice can remediate many deficits. With extra effort a child can overcome or compensate for a problem. Extra effort implies that practice is needed and confirms that he has a problem. The LD child denies the problem by rejecting the need for extra effort. By this means, he protects himself from dealing with the deeper feeling that he is really stupid.

Discredit Education

Another avoidance is to criticize the school experience. LD students profess that learning is boring and irrelevant. Many do not see education as an opportunity to prepare for the future. Indeed, they prefer not thinking about the future. There are no plans, dreams, or realistic goals.

Infantile fantasy may become fixated. Many clumsy, undersized adolescent LD students insist that they will become professional athletes. To hold onto unrealistic fantasies, never to be tested, confirms that there is no need to prepare for the future and no need for school.

Converting Learning into Behavior Problems

After years of failure and humiliation, many LD students

give up on learning. Yet, they are required to attend school. By turning the classroom into a comedy club, a student can transform himself into the class clown. Acceptance and increased stature in the eyes of peers are positive outcomes. Better a comedian than a dunce. For those lacking a sense of humor, truancy and other forms of behavior problems are options.

Parental Involvement

Parental support is crucial. Parents are required to participate in programs devised to remediate their child's learning problems. Minimally, state laws require parental permission to evaluate problems and place qualifying students into special education programs. Individual Educational Plans (I.E.P.) are devised by the school and approved by the parent. These can entail individual training, small group learning, or consultation with the teacher and an expert. In extreme cases, special education is provided in a contained classroom.

Typically, the efforts of teachers flow out of the classroom into the home. In many situations, assignments are to be completed at home. A wholesome, growth-striving student has no problem taking on these responsibilities. A typical, growth-resistant LD student is not likely to willingly comply. Parents are recruited to monitor or enforce the completion of assignments. It becomes the responsibility of the parents to see that the child meets the requirement. Without intending to do so, the school has lured parents into a trap. The personal growth problem has been converted into conflict with authority. The stage has been set for power struggles, broken promises, disappointment, recriminations, and general ill will. All this serves is the avoidance of the real problem—the student's fear of risking that he will once again be humiliated.

No greater challenge faces parents than raising a growth-resistant child. It is distressing and frustrating to observe a child who avoids growth. Often a parent is a scapegoat and drawn into the turmoil of the child's unhappy life. Issues never seem to get resolved. A parent is tempted to take responsibility for the child's growth—as if she can force him to grow up. Power struggles perpetuate the problem. There can be no winners.

A parent who assumes responsibility for her child's growth must manage his life. She provides close supervision, defines needs, structures priorities, and dispenses rewards and punishments. She becomes an adjunct to the school by attending meetings, consulting with teachers, and trying to ensure the child follows the rules.

While such parenting may help a compliant or submissive student, it is fraught with hazards. It fosters dependency and increases the potential for authority conflicts. A child is cast into a role which sows the seeds of rebellion. A parent invested in rescue commits herself to considerable time and effort. As a single, working mom, she can be easily thwarted. She is not around to enforce rules and regulations. It is easy for the child to manipulate and sabotage her efforts to rescue him. This is not the recommended approach for parenting a growth-resistant LD child.

Nor is it recommended that a parent throw in the towel and disregard the child's irresponsibility. If left entirely on his own, the child is vulnerable to develop a potentially self-destructive lifestyle. While in the short-run, conflict can be avoided, in the long-run a parent will be entangled with a child who is psychologically dependent.

Of course, it is necessary to be involved. But, it is a matter of how. To avoid traps, goals must be clear and emotions kept under control. A parent must keep in mind that even the most growth-resistant LD child has a side that strives to grow up. The parent must align with that side of the child's personality. There are four key aspects to this approach.

- Frame issues in terms of responsibility—never doing for him what he can do for himself. For example, parents wake their son in the morning. He claims to be oblivious to every stimulus. But if he is to lead a normal life, he will have to learn to get up by himself or face the consequences of being late to school.

- The parent acknowledges the child has choices and points out differences between mature and immature choices. The parent recognizes and rewards mature choices.

- The parent helps the child see current challenges in terms of possible future results. It is not the parents wrath, but the loss of opportunity that should concern the child.

- The parent monitors the size of growth steps so that the child is not overwhelmed or underchallenged. Many LD students cannot organize well, remember details, or keep track of time. It is important not to expect too much.

The risk is that the child may fail. Failure assaults the ego and communicates a lack of ability. It makes sense to avoid activities that one is unable to master. But education is too important to abandon so easily. Many children do lack ability. However, attitude, effort, and study habits are part of the equation too. While many LD students fear they are stupid, they are capable of learning. Some are intellectually gifted.

Good can be extracted from failure if the student is confronted with the real reasons for it. He has failed because he chose to fail, not because he is stupid. He has failed because he is afraid to dream, formulate goals, and work to realize them. Without goals, school has no meaning. What is the point of conjugating verbs, solving for x, or mastering the periodic table? If he can learn this from his failure, he has given himself a future.

Adolescence

The adolescent's slow severance of the emotional ties to his family, his fearful or exhilarated entrance into the new life which beckons him, these experiences are among the profoundest in human existence.
        Peter Blos, *On Adolescents*, 1962

Adolescence is intense and confusing not only for teenagers but also for parents. This developmental stage brings turmoil and crises into the lives of many. The forces of nature, in combination with psychological and social stresses, can be overwhelming. Parents contend not only with their teenagers, but often with reawakened unresolved issues from their own adolescence. This complicates and confounds responses to the needs of the teenager.

Throughout this discussion, our theme has been that psychological growth is a matter of choice, guided by an internalized map, the Adult Ideal. During childhood the concept of the adult evolves and deepens through actual experiences with adults and adults presented by the media and fantasy play. Response to growth opportunity is also determined by the sense of whether or not success is anticipated at the next level of development. A confident child, with a mature, articulated Adult Ideal is ready to wholesomely respond to the challenges, temptations, and demands of adolescence. In a sense, the future is now. Adolescence is more than experimentation and playing adult roles. The adolescent has developed the physical and sexual potential to actuate fantasy into real life events that impact on himself and others over the course of a lifetime.

The articulation of the Adult Ideal assumes importance for adolescents. This internal Adult Ideal guides judgment and behavior. A young child envisions the adult to be a powerful, brave hero. Two-dimensional cartoon characters are depicted as adults by the media. Unfortunately, the most shallow, immature behavior is presented to children as adult. Is there anything more absurd than labeling pornography and violent fantasy as adult entertainment. These depictions are a far cry from what a serious adult considers mature adulthood. Qualities of moderation, emotional control, consideration for others, investment in serious matters, self-reliance, effort toward future goals, and dependability are not emphasized in these presentations. Unless an adolescent has had direct experience with adults who manifest such qualities, he will not be a part of this internal concept of adulthood. An adolescent body with an infantile sense of adulthood is a potential disaster.

Adolescents who smoke, drink, use drugs, engage in promiscuous sex, and defy authority believe they are being adult. Their dress and manners imitate their model of

adulthood. They strive to be adult. Unless there is expo-
sure to the deeper and broader aspects of adulthood, they
can be adult only in a limited way.

Contemporary American culture is unlikely to provide
better guideposts to developing adolescents who age, but
do not mature. One gets the impression that a goodly segment of the American public has not progressed too far
along many developmental lines. Problems of dependency
and irresponsibility are social consequences of individuals
arrested in personality growth. This evidence suggests
that in large numbers, Americans fail to mature along important developmental lines.

Individual cases suggest, however, that many immature, irresponsible teenagers reverse these patterns and begin taking the steps they resisted in the past.

Eddie was an adolescent during the turmoil of the sixties.
The only child of a tempestuous, alcoholic father and a
gentle, patient mother, his life at home was unstable and
abusive. The clashing temperaments of father and son
generated conflict and violence. Mother feared for the
safety of both. The social and political temper of the
times provided a stage for acting-out defiant, rebellious,
anti-establishment attitudes. A political activist, abuser of
illegal substances, and petty criminal, Eddie's prospects
were bleak. He was asked to leave home.

He lived marginally in San Francisco. Befriended by
older family friends, he survived. He discovered a talent
for working with his hands and supported himself as a
furniture finisher. Then he began designing furniture—
beautiful pieces. He was an artistic success and the
money he earned was invested in northern California real
estate. He married and is the father of two adolescent
children. Eddie had his share of setbacks and adolescent

lapses. But for an adolescent with such bleak prospects, he constructed a meaningful and successful life.

The positive turn in Eddie's life defies common sense. Clearly, the depth of his adolescent turmoil portended future disaster. A life of crime, substance abuse, and disturbed personal relationships would have been no surprise. We assume that patterns are set, doors closed, attitudes established and identifications fixated during adolescence. If these assumptions tell the complete story, Eddie's future was determined and the reversal in his life course remains a mystery. However, this view overlooks factors that exerted positive influence.

Despite the ongoing turmoil, Eddie's parents remained supportive and involved. Their relationship was redefined but not terminated. By stepping out of the supervisory and direct care roles, ongoing family strife was reduced. An interim period of transition into an independent lifestyle was supported by an adult family friend. He dealt with Eddie's agitation without escalating it. As it subsided, Eddie's talents found wholesome expression, personal satisfaction, and financial remunerations. They became a central organizing factor in his professional and social life. Without them, Eddie would have missed the opportunity to meet a wholesome woman capable of coping with his negative excesses.

Parental acceptance, a period of transition aided by his older friend, the development of personal talents, and a wholesome relationship all contributed to Eddie salvaging his life.

By age twelve, Laura was a mess. She is an adopted child who rampaged her way into adolescence. Strong willed and arrogant, there was no limit to her outrageous behavior. She out-gunned and out-maneuvered her parents at every turn. By age fifteen, Laura had run away from several group homes, was hospitalized following a suicide attempt and had dropped out of school. She defied her bigoted, southern mother by dating only black men. She was disowned after she became pregnant. Laura was now dependent on a person whom she distrusted. She lacked the confidence to learn to drive and to complete the G.E.D. Her lifestyle was a natural consequence of a growth-resistant adolescent whose choices reflected low self-esteem and an immature concept of adulthood. By age twenty, her relationship was intact and she was the mother of two children. Laura learned to drive, completed her G.E.D, and landed a job. Her younger child had survived a serious congenital condition and this seemed to strengthen her.

Laura survived adolescence by transforming from a destructive adolescent into a serious young adult. An alienated, rebellious child acting out a sense that she was unwanted, she then committed herself to her children. The caring and protecting she provides them gives meaning to her life and, perhaps, compensates for what was missing for her. Laura was assisted by her therapist who maintained an accepting relationship despite her outrageous behavior. Rejecting parents, teachers, and other adults, Laura continues to call her therapist for support and advice. Neither friends nor parents could provide a sense of balance and perspective. Her therapist can. Laura's story indicates that no matter how rejecting and disparaging adolescence may be, the need for adult influence remains important.

Rudy was an exceptionally bright seventeen year old who failed his junior year and dropped out in his senior year. He lived to party each weekend. The intervening days

were a void. He was interested in nothing. Rudy was alienated from his parents and from his younger sister. He
was contemptuous, emotionally cold, and intellectually
constricted. His fantasy of the good life was to be the toy
boy of a wealthy older woman. His impulse to grow was
weak.

Rudy wanted his own apartment and he demanded that
his father subsidize him. He saw this as a reasonable re-
quest and he was furious when father declined. His father
was a businessman, and Rudy was not in a good position
to negotiate. It would enhance his position to pass the
G.E.D. test, take the S.A.T., apply to college and get a
job. These ideas had been rejected in the past. But as potential bargaining chips they made sense. Rudy is now in
an honors program at a state university.

Rudy's insistence that his father subsidize his irresponsible lifestyle derived from his immature attitudes. A three
year old is entitled, makes demands, and has tantrums
should he not get his way. His therapist helped Rudy to
accept that this level of attitude would lead him nowhere.
By accepting a more mature and cooperating, willingness
to do his share and negotiation, would his prospects improve. Despite his intentions, Rudy had maneuvered himself toward psychological growth. Its symbol, the
apartment, could be attained only by demonstrating maturity.

In each of these cases, parents had lost effectiveness to
guide and influence choices. Indeed, their status was so
low that parental intervention was counter-productive.
Nevertheless, these adolescents remained open to alternative adult sources. The influence of supportive, accepting
adults who manifested attractive qualities enabled them
to accept stabilizing guidance and to incorporate some of

the values of mature adulthood. This suggests the importance of surrogate adults in the lives of adolescents. Be it aunt, uncle, coach, teacher, friend, or therapist, adolescents can often accept from surrogates what they reject from their parents. The relationship must be special to adolescents. If these adolescents perceive caring and commitment they can continue the process of articulating the Adult Ideal, despite long periods in which infantile impressions remained fixated.

As children mature and develop responsible lives, corresponding shifts occur in the nature of parenting. A parent of a wholesome adolescent can begin to relinquish supervisory and enforcement functions. The values that the adolescent has incorporated will guide his choices. This enables a transition in the parent-adolescent relationship. A sense of mutuality and equality develops. The competency of the adolescent is matched by parental pride and enjoyment. A capacity for sharing important experiences enhances a new sense of intimacy. This does not imply that the adolescent will share everything. A progression from parent-child to adult-adult relationship is satisfying. A parent gradually releases the adolescent with the confidence that he will thrive and manage his own life. The parent remains involved as mentor, confidante, and financial aid officer.

A parent of a growth-resistant teenager is stuck. Inevitably, immature choices drag her into his life. How frustrating to be called at work by the attendance officer, to endlessly consult with teachers, to attend therapy sessions, appear before judges, or find the house trashed in an unauthorized party. Such are the lives of parents of growth-resistant adolescents. They are not the innocent victims of bad seeds, for quite often parents have contributed to the situation that entraps them. But neither they nor their offspring deserve to endure the agony.

I urge parents not to give up on their children no matter how desperate the situation may seem. But they should honestly reassess what is and what is not working for them. At least, they can try something new. The merry-go-round goes around and around until someone jumps off. A parent is obliged to seek new approaches for coping with recalcitrant problems. No technique or theory encompasses all phenomena. It is a matter of seeking, rethinking, and experimenting that will lead one out of the morass and remedy impossible situations.

Childhood Asthma

Taught at an early age that they are different—and consistently reminded of this fact—many people with a chronic physical abnormality live out their lives as confused, frustrated and lonely individuals.

Thomas L. Creer and Walter P. Christian,
Chronically Ill and Handicapped Children, 1976

Mother Nature can be unkind. Birth defects, illnesses, accidents, genetic anomalies influence the mental and physical potentialities of a human being. Some effects are so profound that the prospects for growth, no less than for life are guarded. Challenges facing children and families can be overwhelming. Life is not fair. It is tempting to rail against fate, to wallow in bitterness, to succumb to self-pity. Some learn to exploit limitations in ways that are unwholesome. The secondary gain of an illness decreases the will to strive, overcome, and triumph. Growth striving is extinguished. One settles for a constricted life of dependency, devoid of challenge.

Childhood asthma affects ten million people in the United States. Of these, three million are children. The medical and psychological stresses are extraordinary. Some children are greatly debilitated by the condition. Others lead effective and gratifying lives.

Severe asthma is life threatening. In 1988, there were 4600 asthma related deaths. A child's struggle to breathe is a terrible experience, even in its milder forms. Nervous parents are vigilant to a fault. A crib is moved into the parent's bedroom to better monitor the child's breathing. Fear and anxiety are transmitted to the child. Hospitalizations, emergency room visits, appointments with doctors, are painful and frightening procedures.

It is not possible to maintain a carefree childhood. The illness propels a child into a medical culture at the expense of normal childhood activity. Play, running, and jumping may be severely restricted. The child ruefully notices his inability to do what others are able to do. At the first sign of trouble, he is sent home from school. He senses himself as vulnerable and is defined by his illness.

The implications for psychological growth are clear. Independence and exploration are restricted. Parental overprotection is evident. Insecurity, vulnerability, and despair erode self-confidence. The stigma of illness and side effects of medication complicate peer relationships. Education is impeded by frequent absences. Ordinary childhood experiences, essential for normal development, are limited for the asthmatic child.

Potential for maladaptive coping is high. At one extreme are children who deny the seriousness of the illness. They ignore early warning signs, preferring to "tough it out" when they begin to get tight. They are often unreliable about following the medical plan. Their irresponsibility maximizes the risk that a minor episode will evolve into a major attack.

At the other extreme are children debilitated beyond the objective severity of their illness. They are overly cautious and may use the illness to avoid stresses and challenges. They develop a fearful attitude about life. Their vulnerability is a central component of their sense of self.

It is, of course, possible to develop a mature, responsible personality and to lead a gratifying life no matter how severe the asthma. Many have done so. To master the illness, one accepts its realities, minimizes its impact by taking medical precaution, leads a health enhancing life, and finds meaning in other aspects of life. It is not easy for children with early onset asthma to learn these lessons.

The growth perspective emphasizes choice. Children with asthma are confronted with choices weighted with extraordinary risk. Experiences necessary to progress along developmental lines are fraught with perceived and real danger.

The issue of separation illustrates the problem. While difficult for many children, this developmental task is more so for the asthmatic who depends on a parent to assess respiration and to medicate as needed. The presence of the parent is reassuring and a key component of the security system. Substantial anxiety will have to be overcome for the child to function independently of the parent.

Separation and independence requires confidence that the child is competent to manage his own illness. He monitors his own respiratory status and knows the steps to take to stop problems at an early stage. It requires the courage to avoid potentially dangerous activity and comply with the treatment plan; thereby, risking the ridicule of peers. If a twelve year old boy is afraid to use an inhaler at school because classmates may laugh at him, it will be difficult for child and parent to initiate the process of separation.

School, athletics, sibling relations, and fantasy life are the arenas for personality growth. In each, there are special problems for the asthmatic child.

School

Asthma is a leading cause of school absence. A parent is faced with a difficult decision when a child wheezes or complains of tightness in the morning. A fine line exists between illness and stress related to other factors. To function when feeling less than 100 percent is important. But minimizing early warning signs can aggravate the condition. The consequences of mistaken judgment can be serious. The conservative approach is to keep the child home.

Absence impacts several dimensions of growth. Academic performance is compromised increasing tendencies to avoid frustrating school experiences. The stigma of illness and absence complicates peer relationships. Heightened stress promotes avoidance tendencies. It is tough to return to school after an illness.

A child who develops symptomotology in school is referred to the nurse. School policies are determined to avoid risk and liability. With a time out and warm water, symptoms may remit and the child returns to the classroom. Why take the chance? The child is sent home.

Parents can advocate on behalf of their child. They take a leading role in insisting that they, their child, the school, and physician collaborate. The goal is to maximize educa-

tional participation without exposing the child to undue
risk. It is important to define medical reality and to de-
vise a plan to guide parental and school decision making
in response to complaints or signs of illness.

Athletics

Participation in sports programs benefits asthmatic children. It provides opportunities to join peers in fun activities, to test physical limits, to respond realistically to
problems, should they develop. Allowances are often necessary. Many coaches maintain a tough-it-out philosophy
and want to push a child to dangerous limits. They need
to be educated. Some have rigid attitudes. If a coach is unable to appreciate the seriousness of the problem, find another team.

Non-competitive sports such as biking, hiking, and swimming provide similar benefits. These activities have the advantage of helping a child to respond to emergency
situations. High in the mountains or on the bike trail, difficulties may occur. The child can learn proper techniques
to control panic and care for himself.

Sibling Complications

A sick child requires time, energy, and attention. The impact on healthy siblings is considerable. Time devoted to
the care of the asthmatic child is not available to them.
They too have needs. Many healthy children have ambivalent feelings toward the ill sibling. While compassionate
and tender, they resent the attention he receives. Their
strength and health work against them. They feel cheated
for being healthy. If weak or ill, one receives parental attention and support. Growth trends are reversed. Rather
than welcoming the experiences that nurture growth striv-

ing, growth resistance is increased. Illness is used to manipulate and control events, to gain advantage. While the healthy sibling develops maladaptive behavior to shift the balance of influence. Harried parents are trapped and lose perspective.

Professional guidance can be beneficial to families coping with the complexities inherent in raising a child with a chronic illness. Stresses and burdens can be overwhelming. Maladaptive coping is contagious. The strengthening potential of adversity is bypassed.

Fantasy

Early onset asthma confronts a child with the dark, devastating side of life. Psychological defenses are insufficient to shield the child from the fears and stresses. Trauma, life threatening experience, emergencies, and reduced airflow are incorporated in the fantasy life. It is not a matter of, "When I grow up, I'll be. . . ." but, "If I grow up, . . ."

> Although he was only four and a half years old, Jordy had been hospitalized on several occasions, was often rushed to the emergency room and was taking medication that caused irritability. He was temperamental, obstinate and aggressive toward his older, healthy sister. Despite intense medical effort, his asthma was poorly controlled. He was referred for play therapy.

> For months, he played only one game on a weekly basis. The doll house was neatly arranged and a set of plastic beads fitted into a line about three feet long. This was a space snake that swooped down on the doll house. The furniture and dolls were thrown about in fury and chaos. When it seemed that all was lost, a superhero arrived. An epic battle ensued. Bead by bead, the space snake was dismantled, the family rescued. The struggle had barely con-

cluded when another snake attacked the house. The game played out, again and again.

The therapist told Jordy that the space snake was his asthma.

He feared that it would kill him and destroy the family. The superhero was his doctor, who would always arrive to save him. He could stop the attack, but could not prevent the next one. Jordy listened quietly.

The following session, Jordy announced that he wanted to play football. He never again played the game at the doll house. At the end of his therapy Jordy told his parents, "I used to be afraid of my asthma, but I'm not afraid anymore." His mother was stunned. He had never revealed in words how afraid he had been.

Jordy had learned to master his fear and to turn his attention to ordinary childhood interests. His illness assumed a peripheral, not a central role in his life. Several years later, Jordy visited me. He was fun, cheerful, just a kid. He seemed to be growing normally.

Asthma and other chronic illnesses are adversities that no one relishes. Children ask, "Why me?" Some see it as a gift from God, a special challenge to help bring out the best in them. Others are philosophical, bitter or despairing. The potential for growth is hidden in the anguish and difficulty. Parents can help a child discover a gratifying life.

Final Thoughts

Every hand's a winner and every hand's a loser claims Kenny Rogers in his song *The Gambler*. In life, the cards are dealt at birth by Mother Nature. The lucky ones receive good hands; a full house, straight, or royal flush. These children are blessed with healthy, attractive bodies, high IQs, athletic ability, loving parents who are family oriented with strong parenthood values. It is no great accomplishment to develop fully when dealt such a hand. Yet, many fail to win, despite their good cards. They remain vain, selfish, and immature. They make poor choices and trap themselves in ungratifying, shallow existences. More interesting are those who win with weak hands. Jack high or two pair are not much with which to play. Average or less in genetic qualities, environmentally disadvantaged, chronically ill, deprived or unlucky, they grow to be mature, productive individuals. They have faced the challenges and they have won. We have much to learn from them.

The last person to cross the finish line, not the winner of the marathon is the more interesting and triumphant. The winner is surely to be admired. She has developed her gifts through hard work and dedication. She was dealt high cards and played them well. She deserves to win.

The last place finisher did not hold the cards. He doesn't have a chance, but he ran anyway. Lacking in stamina, strength, and athletic ability, he accepted the challenge to test himself, to experience the excitement of the event, to risk failure and humiliation. Fred Lebow ran the New York Marathon following surgery to remove a cancerous brain tumor. His running partner was Grete Waitz, the woman's champion. The winners of this race were showered and relaxed by the time Grete and Fred crossed the finish line. They embraced in tearful triumph. Grete had won nine times. But running with Fred was the truer measure of her humanity. Fred's triumph not only revealed his courage, but ennobled all who confront adversity.

Norman Croucher was a child who enjoyed climbing the granite outcrops dotting the country side of Cornwall, England. In the town square was a statue of Forbisher, the famous 18th century seafarer. Norman dreamed of traveling the world and climbing mountains. Not a serious student, his best grades were for effort. But Norman was smart enough to go to college. A gregarious fellow he drank too much at a local pub. Staggering home, he fell off an embankment onto a railroad track. The train was unable to stop in time. When Norman regained consciousness, he found that his legs were gone. "I have no one to blame but myself, was his first thought."

His dream persisted. But Norman had to find new means to make it come true. Prosthetic devices were becoming available. Norman was fitted with artificial legs, controlled by nerve impulses. He demonstrated their effectiveness by hiking the length of Britain, 900 miles. Norman was a national hero. Later, he led parties on treks though the Alps, the Himalayas, and the Andes.

Learning disabled, latchkey, asthmatic children and all the others who live in difficult circumstances can grow successfully. Parents can help them to find the way. Every hand's a winner and every hand's a loser. To make the most of life, to develop full potential, to overcome adversity, to give back in kindness, and to enjoy the ride is all that we ask of ourselves. We can ensure that the parenthood card that we deal to our children is high. Some are better, some worse. We control only one card. Let it not be one that the player, our child, will want to discard. We want the parenthood card to be the one around which a winning hand is constructed.

Index

Moving With Children: A Parent's Guide To Moving With Children

Thomas Olkowski, Ph.D. and Lynn Parker, LCSW
ISBN 1-880197-08-1, softcover, 196 pages, $12.95
Moving. . . helps parents understand and deal with the many feelings and behaviors of children when families move. Practical and effective suggestions to help families deal with the various stages of moving—from planning and discussing the move with their children to saying goodbye, packing and unpacking, exploring the new community, meeting new friends, and settling into the new home. Resources, Bibiolgraphy, Illustrations, Index.

Helper: Real Stories of Welfare and Probation

Sonya Jason
ISBN 1-880197-09-X, softcover, $12.95, 158 pages
Helper shows what doesn't work and what needs to change in two of society's most costly civilian bureaucracies, welfare and probation. *Helper* is a series of vignettes about people and situations as seen through the eyes of the author who as a social worker and probation officer spent years working with people and the bureaucracies that were suppose to help them. The stories depict the wonder and diversity of human beings and the looniness of bureaucracies determined to fit people into rigid slots and deal with them accordingly. Sometimes the people are amusing, sometimes dangerous.

Dear Larissa: Sexuality Education for Girls Ages 11-17

Cynthia G. Akagi
ISBN 1-880197-10-3, softcover, $12.95, 242 pages
A book for mothers (fathers) to give to their daughters. It is a mother's letters to her daughter about growing up—body changes, menstruation, boys, dating, love and sex— with space for personal comments. *Dear Larissa* helps parents and daughters build communication in a caring manner. Illustrations, Glossary, Bibliography, Index.

Cooking With Tofu: For Those Who Hate Tofu But Don't Know Any Better

Robert W. McBride
ISBN 1-880197-01-4, spiral bound, $7.95, 62 pages
Tofu versions of everybody's favorite "cheating " foods: French toast, burgers, fries, thousand island dressing, "cheese" balls, tacos—even jerky and chocolate creme pie.

Prices valid in the United States only and subject to change without notice.

These best sellers are available in your bookstore or order by calling, toll-free, **1-800-828-0113** to use your Visa/MasterCard.

Mail orders must include *complete payment* (check or Visa/MasterCard number with expiration date) unless you are a government agency, college, library or another official public organization, in which case please include a purchase order number.

Include $2.00 for shipping & handling with each order.
Colorado residents need to also include 3.8% sales tax.

To ensure your order is properly handled, include the name and quantity of each title, your complete name and shipping address and complete payment. Thank you.

Send orders to: GYLANTIC PUBLISHING CO.   (303) 797-6093
                    P. O. Box 2792   Fax:(303) 727-4279
                    Littleton, CO 80161-2792   E-mail: GylanP@aol.com